D1511917

Conservation Heroes

ANSEL
ADAMS

Conservation Heroes

Ansel Adams

John James Audubon

Rachel Carson

Jacques Cousteau

Jane Goodall

Al Gore

Steve and Bindi Irwin

Chico Mendes

John Muir

Theodore Roosevelt

Conservation Heroes

ANSEL ADAMS

Krista West

CHELSEA HOUSE
An Infobase Learning Company

Chelsea House
An imprint of Infobase Learning
132 West 31st Street
New York, NY 10001

Library of Congress Cataloging-in-Publication Data
West, Krista.
  Ansel Adams / by Krista West.
      p. cm. — (Conservation heroes)
  Includes bibliographical references and index.
  ISBN 978-1-60413-946-4 (hardcover)
   1. Adams, Ansel, 1902–1984—Juvenile literature. 2. Photographers—United
States—Biography—Juvenile literature. I. Title.
  TR140.A3W47 2010
  333.72092—dc22
  [B]   2010030591

Chelsea House books are available at special discounts when purchased in
bulk quantities for businesses, associations, institutions, or sales promotions.
Please call our Special Sales Department in New York at (212) 967-8800 or
(800) 322-8755.

You can find Chelsea House on the World Wide Web
at http://www.chelseahouse.com

Text design by Annie O'Donnell
Cover design by Takeshi Takahashi
Composition by Newgen North America
Cover printed by Bang Printing, Brainerd, MN
Book printed and bound by Bang Printing, Brainerd, MN
Date printed: February 2011
Printed in the United States of America

10 9 8 7 6 5 4 3 2 1

This book is printed on acid-free paper.

All links and Web addresses were checked and verified to be correct at the time
of publication. Because of the dynamic nature of the Web, some addresses and
links may have changed since publication and may no longer be valid.

Contents

Love at First Sight

Way too excited to sleep, 14-year-old Ansel Adams was up before the sun. Hours before breakfast, he was wandering around in the small town of El Portal, California. He and his parents, Charles and Olive Adams, were waiting to board an open-air bus that would take them 10 miles (16 kilometers) and 2,000 feet (610 meters) into the heart of the Yosemite Valley. This vast stretch of wilderness is located at the western end of California's Sierra Nevada Mountains. It was June 1916, and it was Ansel's first trip into wild lands.

Prior to this long-anticipated summer morning, Ansel got a sneak preview of Yosemite in a book. He was eager to see it all for himself, and he had no idea of the enormous impact this place would have on his life and career. On this first visit to the Yosemite Valley, Ansel would fall in love at first sight with the beauty of the land. That love changed the course of his life.

THE BOOK

Ansel Adams was not a healthy child. The gangly, lonely, energetic young Ansel was often sick in bed. In early 1916, when Ansel was 14 years old and trapped in bed by a bad cold, his Aunt Mary brought him some of her own books to read while resting. One was her copy of *In the Heart of the Sierras.* First published in 1888, this book contained a complete look at all things Yosemite, including the area's history, illustrations of its now-famous places and trails, and travel tips.

MARY BRAY ADAMS (1864–1944)

Mary Bray Adams—known to Ansel simply as Aunt Mary—was the unmarried, younger sister of Ansel's mom, Olive Bray. She was the first person to introduce Ansel to Yosemite National Park.

Aunt Mary and her aging father came to live with the Adamses in San Francisco in 1908, shortly after Mary's mother died. Neither had any money or form of income, so Ansel's father supported Mary and Grandpa Bray (as Ansel called him) financially until their deaths. (Grandpa Bray died in 1919, and Aunt Mary in 1944.) Aunt Mary was a proper woman, fond of poetry and reading, and likely assisted in Ansel's homeschool education when Charles pulled him out of school in 1914.

In early 1916, Aunt Mary loaned Ansel *In the Heart of the Sierras,* by J.M. Hutchings. The book, arguably, changed the life of Ansel Adams, launching him into a lifelong love of Yosemite before he even set foot in the mountains. She was clearly an influential person in his life. Yet beyond this single, contained action, little is known about Aunt Mary's personality and passions.

The letters Ansel wrote to his father from Yosemite reveal as much about Aunt Mary as anything. In June 1920, for example, Aunt

Ansel pored over the pages of the book repeatedly. "The text is florid, commonplace, and not too accurate, but I did not know that—I devoured every word and pored over the pages many times," he wrote in *Ansel Adams: An Autobiography,* published in 1985.

Ansel was hooked, as he was already prone to long, solo walks exploring the sand dunes near his home at the western edge of San Francisco. He was immediately absorbed by the book's description

Mary stayed with Ansel in the park for a short time. In a lengthy letter to his father that month, which was later published in *Ansel Adams: Letters and Images 1916–1984,* Ansel relays a brief update on Aunt Mary:

> Aunt Mary has not been feeling well for the last two days, she was quite upset and throwing up her toes yesterday but feels somewhat better today. When asked how she feels and when cautioned to take it easy and rest all I can get out of her is "sugar" or "pshaw" and you know when she goes that far into profanity she means something by it.

This visual, funny description of a contained Aunt Mary is typical of Ansel's clear and colorful letter-writing style.

Much of what history knows about Aunt Mary and Ansel's relationships with friends and foes comes from the vast pool of his own words. Over his lifetime, Ansel wrote thousands of letters and postcards to family, friends, photographers, and politicians. If the library of his letters is an accurate reflection of his correspondence, he apparently wrote more letters to his Aunt Mary than to his mother during the many summers he spent in Yosemite.

of a new kind of wilderness. The mountains, valleys, and waterways of Yosemite were unlike anything Ansel had seen or heard of before.

Young Ansel, an only child, soon began to lobby his upper-class parents for a family vacation to Yosemite, only 150 miles (240 km) from San Francisco, but a two-day journey then. Aunt Mary, who lived with the Adams family, refused to leave her cat, Blinkers, unattended on such a long trip (even though a neighbor agreed to watch the cat). Olive, Ansel's mom, thought Yellowstone was much too far away to be worth the trouble. Yet Charles Adams was accustomed to catering to his only son. Eventually, they all gave in to Ansel's nonstop pleadings.

THE FIRST VISIT

On June 1, 1916, Ansel, Charles, and Olive Adams caught the Southern Pacific train in Oakland, California, to begin the family's first journey to Yosemite National Park. They would take this train to the small town of Merced (a route that is still traveled by rail today). There they would transfer to the Yosemite Valley Railroad (which was replaced by a road in 1926) to follow the Merced River to the town of El Portal. From there, travelers boarded an open-air bus for the bumpy ride into the valley.

At the time, people dressed formally to travel. Men wore hats and heavy jackets; women wore blouses, long skirts, bloomers, hats, and high boots. Such proper travel attire was unbearably hot during the summer in California. Ansel, however, was largely unfazed by the heat because he was so excited and so determined to see the Yosemite he had seen in his book. In March 1980, Ansel Adams recounted the journey to the Wilderness Society, a wilderness protection organization that he worked and wrote for later in his life:

> All day long we rode, over the Coast Range . . . down across the heat-shimmering San Joaquin Valley, up through the even hotter foothills to the threshold of Yosemite. I can still feel the furnace blasts of air buffeting through the coaches, and hear the pounding, roaring exhaust of the locomotive reechoing from the steep walls of the Merced Canyon.

The colorful beauty of Yosemite National Park is reflected in the Merced River.

As a teen, Ansel Adams first saw Yosemite and was fascinated by its majestic mountains, carved valleys, and vast forestland.

The Yosemite Valley Railroad car was full of dust and people—elders, inquisitive children, and impatient parents—but the air was clean and clear. Ansel could see the distant mountains of Yosemite from 100 miles (160 km) away. His anticipation grew with every new view that came into sight.

At the end of a long day, the train stopped in El Portal, a very small town by the Merced River on the western edge of Yosemite National Park. Here, the Adams family spent the night at the luxurious Del Portal Hotel awaiting the open-air bus that would take them into the heart of the park. "After an ample meal we were called to the huge, open bus that provided gales of fresh air, mixed with dust, fumes, and wonderful views," he wrote in his 1985 autobiography. "We finally emerged at Valley View—the splendor of Yosemite burst upon us and it was glorious."

Young Ansel was simply consumed by the land around him despite being covered in dust and a bit nauseous from the drive along the curvy, bumpy, steep dirt roads. "One wonder after another descended upon us," he wrote in his autobiography. "I recall not only the colossal but the little things: the grasses and ferns, cool atriums of the forest . . . There was light everywhere!"

Ansel wanted to look in every direction at the same time. Many of the sites were familiar to him from Aunt Mary's book, particularly Yosemite's El Capitan, Bridalveil Falls, and Half Dome. Then Charles Adams interrupted Ansel's sensory overload and presented him with an unexpected gift.

THE FIRST CAMERA

Shortly after the family's arrival in Yosemite Valley, Ansel's parents surprised him with a simple camera—a Kodak Box Brownie. Introduced in 1900, Brownie cameras were the first inexpensive (they cost $1 to $2 at the time), portable cameras that allowed almost anyone to easily take lots of snapshots. After just a few minutes of instruction, this simple camera gave Ansel a way to channel his hyperactive excitement for Yosemite. He immediately began taking pictures of the world around him and sharing the beauty of the land with others.

In a letter to Aunt Mary dated June 23, 1916, Ansel wrote, "I am sending you two pictures of Yosemite Valley that I have taken. Films are expensive to develop and I expect to be broke if I keep up the rate I am taking pictures. I have taken 30 already."

(continues on page 16)

CHEAT SHEET: THE YOSEMITE VALLEY

The Yosemite Valley has long been recognized as a unique and valuable place. Many of its popular sites have become major tourist destinations.

Many native peoples lived in the Yosemite Valley for centuries before American explorers even set foot in the place. The valley naturally provided a wealth of nuts, berries, and small game as food, as well as mountains and valleys to serve as protective shelters from weather and invaders. When the first Americans arrived in large numbers, about 200 Ahwahnechee people occupied the land.

With the rise of the California Gold Rush in the 1850s, an estimated 300,000 more Americans moved into California. The population of San Francisco exploded and explorers trickled into Yosemite in search of gold. Spats, raids, and robberies between the newcomers and the Ahwahnechee increased. Eventually, the governor of California ordered an end to the conflict. A series of battles known as the Mariposa Wars followed, and the Ahwahnechee were not so peacefully moved to a reservation near Fresno, California, around 1860.

The federal government first recognized Yosemite's worth in 1864. On June 30 of that year, President Abraham Lincoln signed a bill to create the Yosemite Grant, the first law that set aside an area of land specifically for preservation and public use. Yosemite was the first wild place in the United States to be protected and made accessible to the public.

In the early years of the Yosemite Grant, major efforts were made to make public access to Yosemite easier. A railroad was built in 1869, three stagecoach roads were constructed in the 1870s, and much was written and publicized about the place. With the increased traffic, it didn't take long before concern over issues such as logging and sheep grazing grew, and new efforts to protect the area from tourists took shape.

In 1916 the National Park Service was formed, and the area protected by the Yosemite Grant became more like the national park known today. Much happened during that year: The primitive Tioga Pass Road was finished (the highest roadway in California at 9,943 feet or 3,031 m), the Tuolumne Meadows Lodge was built (along the new Tioga Road), and two new campgrounds were created. It was also then that Ansel Adams arrived to get his first view of the park.

Today, many of the park's destinations are commonly known, and many of these places were first popularized by Adams's famous photographs. The following are just a few of the Yosemite sites that Ansel Adams often visited and photographed.

- **Bridalveil Falls** A waterfall, 620 feet (188 m) tall, located near the entrance of the Yosemite Valley. The Ahwahnechee believed the falls, which flow year round, were home to a spirit that guarded the entrance to the valley.
- **El Capitan** A vertical, granite rock formation on the northern side of the valley, rising 3,000 feet (910 m). American explorers named the formation "the captain" in 1851.
- **Half Dome** Arguably Yosemite's most familiar site, this granite crest soars 4,737 feet (1,444 m) above the eastern end of the valley floor. Its image appears on the California state quarter.
- **Yosemite Falls** The highest flowing waterfall in North America at 1,430 feet (436 m). According to Ahwahnechee legends, a pool at the base of the falls sucked trespassers into its depths.

(continued from page 13)

One of Ansel's many images from this first visit was taken completely by accident. To get a better view of Yosemite's Half Dome, Ansel took his camera and climbed an old tree stump near his family's tent. When perched on top of the stump and about to push the shutter, the stump suddenly crumbled and sent Ansel and the camera tumbling headfirst to the ground. On the way down, Ansel accidentally pushed the shutter on the upside-down camera. Neither

The No. 1 Kodak Box Brownie was Ansel Adams's first camera. Shown here sitting atop its original packaging, the Brownie was made of wood and cardboard and cost $1. It produced square photos.

Yosemite's Half Dome is its most popular rock formation. The granite peak rises more than 4,737 feet (1,444 m) above the valley floor.

Ansel nor the camera was hurt. The film developer later presented Ansel with an uncut sheet of the negative pictures—clearly showing the upside-down image of Half Dome—and asked how this had happened. Ansel explained and later recalled receiving only a strange and doubtful look from the developer. "I do not think he was ever certain of my normalcy from then on," Ansel wrote in his autobiography.

The accidental image is one of Ansel's first pictures of the mountain of which he would take dozens of photos in the course of his lifetime. He didn't think it was too bad for a first attempt. He mounted this and many of his early Yosemite photographs in books he called "photodiaries." These were the precursors to later influential photography books that changed the way people treated the land.

THE IMPACT

Although Ansel liked his early photographs of Yosemite, he realized immediately that they did not convey the power and beauty of the sites he so loved in the park. After his first visit he returned to Yosemite—summer after summer—for the next 11 years to shoot and develop photographs. Over time, these photographs became his life's work. The accidental conservation movement that they inspired became his legacy.

In later years, Ansel Adams traced it all back to his first visit to the Yosemite Valley in 1916. As he told the Wilderness Society in March 1980:

> That first impression of the valley—white water, azaleas, cool fir caverns, tall pines and stolid oaks, cliffs rising to undreamed-of heights, the poignant sounds and smells of the Sierra . . . was a culmination of experience so intense as to be almost painful. From that day in 1916 my life has been colored and modulated by the great earth gesture of the Sierra.

And it all started when he was sick in bed, and his Aunt Mary loaned him a simple book to keep him busy. Little did she realize the door she had opened for Ansel on that day.

A Bumpy Childhood

Ansel Easton Adams was born in his family's San Francisco home on February 20, 1902. From a very early age, he seemed to ingest all the sights and sounds around him. He remembered them later in life. His autobiography and countless interviews are spattered with memories of his early childhood. In almost every case, they involve clear scenes from the surrounding world.

Sometime before he could walk, for example, Ansel remembered lying in his baby crib outside on a warm afternoon, watching fingers of fog blow across a clear blue sky. When the sky became mostly gray, his nanny, Nelly, swooped him up to take him inside.

At age two, he remembered the lights bouncing around his home during a winter party indoors. His mother brought him downstairs to "display him to an audience of black ties, white shirts, high-collared lace dresses, necklaces, rings, generous smiles, and strange sounds," according to Ansel in his autobiography. He remembered closing his eyes to the bright lights and loud sounds.

At age three, he recalled standing at the window of his mother's room and watching the misty rain around the Golden Gate Bridge,

Ansel Adams's hometown of San Francisco offered him plenty of beautiful inspiration. The Golden Gate Bridge, San Francisco Bay, and the sailboats in the bay were among his favorite sights.

a passing sailboat in the San Francisco Bay, and the sand dunes of nearby Marin County. He said he remembered a quiet scene with cool, translucent, natural light.

Ansel Adams was not, it seems, a typical child from the very beginning. He had a knack for noticing and remembering the scenes from the world around him, always paying special attention to the lights and the sounds. He did not have a typical upbringing either. The only son of upper-class parents, Ansel spent much of his time alone, exploring the sand dunes near his home. When he reached school age, it quickly became clear that traditional schooling was not the best fit for him. He didn't learn well or excel in school, and it took some time to find the right path in education.

Many of these childhood bumps were managed and supervised by Ansel's devoted father, Charles Adams. But there was one "bump," when Ansel was just four years old, that his father could not control—the great San Francisco Earthquake of 1906.

THE 1906 EARTHQUAKE

Ansel was awakened at about 5:15 A.M. on April 18, 1906, by a tremendous noise and a shaking bed. His room was violently moving back and forth. The glass of the west window shattered. He watched a brick chimney topple outside his north window. The chaos continued for less than one minute and the house remained largely intact and standing. Though he was just four years old at the time, he vividly remembered the San Francisco earthquake of 1906 later in life.

The earthquake, which many years later the U.S. Geological Survey (USGS) estimated to be a magnitude 7.8, was the deadliest natural disaster in California's history. The main shaking was reportedly felt from Oregon to Los Angeles, and was centered in the new city of San Francisco. Fires, started largely by leaking gas lines, erupted throughout the city after the quake hit. Smaller earthquakes, called aftershocks, rocked the city in the following days. According to the U.S. Geological Society, at least 3,000 people died and there was more than $500 million in property loss. The Adams family was lucky to be alive and to have a house that was still standing.

Prior to one of the aftershocks, Ansel was playing outside in his mother's garden when she called him in for breakfast. As he was walking inside, an aftershock began. The earth shook Ansel off balance, and he smashed his face into a low brick wall surrounding the garden, breaking his nose. His nose bled for hours. By the time a doctor was contacted, Ansel's parents were told to let the nose heal and set it straight when he matured. "Apparently I never matured," Adams later joked in his autobiography, "as I have yet to see a surgeon about it." His crooked, left-leaning nose was a characteristic facial feature in later life.

SCHOOL DAYS

School did not go smoothly for Ansel—socially or academically. He attended many different schools in San Francisco as his parents searched for the right fit for their son. By age 12, he had been in and out of a long line of schools and the family had developed a pattern of dropping a school as soon as things there became difficult, and then moving on to the next problematic place.

At one school, for example, a bully hit Ansel, who returned the hit with a punch to the chin, knocking the bully out cold. The principal took Ansel home personally, stating that fighting was simply not allowed at school. At home, Ansel's mom asked if the bully hurt him. Ansel said yes. She then asked if Ansel hurt the bully. Ansel again said yes. Case closed. The topic was never addressed again. Ansel simply moved on to a new school.

On another occasion, Ansel was sitting in class listening, and suddenly the whole scene seemed terribly funny. Ansel started laughing hysterically, pointing at the teacher, and howling at what he suddenly thought was a ridiculous situation. Again, Ansel was escorted home to his mother. He did not return to that school. "Each day was a severe test for me, sitting in a dreadful classroom

CHARLES HITCHCOCK ADAMS (1868–1951)

Charles Hitchcock Adams is widely credited with nurturing and molding the unusual energy of his only son. Despite inheriting an unwanted career running the family business and coping with the marital stress of lost finances, Charles Adams seemed determined to let Ansel make his own choices. He also seemed determined to fully support the choices that he made.

Charles was the youngest of five children born to Cassandra and William Adams. The New England family settled south of San Francisco in 1857 and built a money-making lumber business called Adams & Blinn. Eventually, the company established lumber mills in Washington and Mississippi, and operated a large fleet of lumber ships. The business made enough money to establish the Adams family as upper-class elites in San Francisco society for a time. But the wealth did not last.

By the time Charles was at the University of California, Berkeley, studying astronomy and chemistry, his father's lumber business was faltering. Charles was discouraged from pursuing his love of nature and strongly persuaded to take over the family business. So instead of pursuing a career in science, Charles Adams became a businessman working for his father. It was a career that he did not want.

The economic depression that followed the 1906 earthquake, combined with mill fires and shipwrecks, crushed the family lumber business. By 1917, Charles Adams had lost most of his family's fortune and his own paycheck. He was forced to take a variety of business jobs, none of which was successful. The resulting loss of money and status became a sore spot that his wife, Olive, never let him forget.

Perhaps because of his unfortunate career and marriage, many suggest that Charles Adams pinned his lost dreams on his only son,

(continues)

(continued)

Ansel, and gave him the freedom and support to pursue his own passions. As director Ric Burns said in his 2002 *Ansel Adams: A Documentary Film,* "Charles H. Adams, a businessman who in his own youth had been discouraged from pursuing a passionate love of nature and science, was determined that his son would be free to follow his own interests, wherever they might lead."

When traditional schooling didn't work for Ansel, Charles paid for tutors in algebra and Greek. When Ansel wanted to visit Yosemite in 1916, Charles took him there. Charles gave Ansel his first camera and responded to his hundreds of letters sent from summers in Yosemite. "He [Charles] just indulged him to an extraordinary degree," said William Turnage, Adams's business manager later in life and the current manager of the Ansel Adams Trust, in *Ansel Adams: A Documentary Film.*

In return, it seems Ansel indulged his father's interests as well. Charles and Ansel spent long evenings studying the night sky together. Though Charles never finished his astronomy education, he did join the Astronomical Society of the Pacific and served as its secretary/treasurer from 1925 to 1950. The Adams crater on the Moon is co-named in honor of Charles Adams.

Charles also loved wildflowers of all sorts. During his summers in Yosemite, Ansel would take pictures of wildflowers and send them back to his father in the city. The flowers were a common topic of conversation in the letters sent between father and son during the summers Ansel spent in the park.

while the sun and fog played outside," he wrote in his autobiography. "Most of the information received meant nothing to me . . . I longed for the outdoors, leaving only a small part of my conscious self to pay attention to schoolwork."

Eventually, Ansel's father decided not to enroll his son in yet another traditional school. Instead, he would keep Ansel at home to study under his own guidance. As film director Ric Burns explains in his 2002 PBS presentation *Ansel Adams: A Documentary Film,* "Abandoning the idea of conventional schooling when the boy was only twelve, his gentle, courtly father, Charles, poured all the love and energy he had into his difficult only son: arranging private tuition in algebra and Greek, and letting him roam for hours along the dunes and cliffs beyond the house—anywhere his boundless energy took him." Thus began Ansel's largely informal and self-led education.

NOT-SO-SCHOOL DAYS

Given the freedom to educate himself, Ansel went outside and collected samples of sand, driftwood, and life all around him. His favorite hobby was collecting insects of all sorts and displaying the tiny corpses on pins in the bottom drawer of the chest in his room. One of his prize specimens was a black beetle, 3 inches (7.6 cm) long, that "always looked ready for takeoff," he wrote in his autobiography. When houseguests stayed in his room, he often had to hide his bug collection in order to provide them a good night's sleep.

Ansel began making daily trips to the dunes near his home to collect more bugs and pieces of driftwood. He collected some driftwood because the pieces were unusual and interesting shapes; other pieces were picked up to be burned for heat in the house. On these trips he would also haul sand home and sprinkle it around on the ground, exploring different patterns and shapes.

In 1915, when Ansel was 13 years old, his informal education took another turn. His father bought him a yearlong pass to the Panama-Pacific International Exposition, a huge world's fair sprawling across 635 acres (657 hectares) of land now known as the Marina in northern San Francisco. Ansel was expected to continue his lessons at home, but spend a good part of each day exploring the fairgrounds.

Over the course of the year, Ansel visited each exhibit many times and got to know many of the people working at the exposition. His father would often meet him in the afternoon and they would explore together. Ansel attended organ concerts in the Festival Hall daily, began demonstrating a new adding machine, learned about the history of typewriters and other machines, and often wandered home very late, tired and exhausted from his free-roaming, exploratory day.

THE PANAMA-PACIFIC INTERNATIONAL EXPOSITION

The Panama-Pacific International Exposition of 1915 was officially a celebration of the completion of the Panama Canal, a human-made seaway joining the Atlantic and Pacific oceans in Central America. The exposition was also the four-hundredth anniversary of the discovery of the Pacific Ocean by Spanish explorer Vasco Núñez de Balboa.

Unofficially, the Panama-Pacific Exposition was a way to help the San Francisco area recover from the aftermath of the 1906 earthquake and fires that destroyed much of the city. About 76 city blocks were cleared and made to set the stage for the exposition. For three years prior to opening, architects and designers went to work creating the new spaces for the exposition. All the buildings were restricted to an eight-color pastel theme, making the final product appear unified.

The Tower of Jewels was the centerpiece of the new construction, serving as the main entrance to the exposition. The building was 435 feet (133 m) tall and decorated with more than 100,000 cut-glass jewels dangling from its sides, blowing in the wind and reflecting lights all around. Inside were painted murals depicting

As an adult, Adams credited much of his success to his father. "I often wonder at the strength and courage my father had in taking me out of the traditional school situation and providing me with these extraordinary learning experiences," he wrote in his 1985 autobiography. "I am certain he established the positive direction of my life that otherwise, given my native hyperactivity, could have been confused and catastrophic. I trace who I am and the direction of my development to those years of growing up at our house on the

Balboa's discovery and the construction of the Panama Canal. It was one of dozens of new buildings made specifically to house the exposition's exhibits.

Eventually, thousands of exhibits opened on exposition grounds, including historical exhibits from different countries, an exhibit from each state in the United States (Pennsylvania sent the Liberty Bell to be exhibited), scientific and medical exhibits, and artistic and musical exhibits. In addition, a large area known as the Zone was full of amusement park rides, games, and international foods.

Many exhibits were designed to sell new things for the home or office. Others were there merely for education. The Palace of Varied Industries, for example, was a hall containing new mechanical gadgets of all sorts, including new styles of sewing machines, new pocket watches, and the latest papermaking tools and techniques.

At the end of each day, a fireworks display would close out the evening. The massive exposition was open from February 20 to December 4, 1915, and was widely considered a success. Almost all of the buildings were torn down at the end of 1915. Only the Palace of Fine Arts was left standing and was reconstructed in the 1960s. It currently holds the Exploratorium, an interactive science museum for the young at heart in San Francisco.

A poster advertises the Panama-Pacific International Exposition, which Ansel Adams eagerly attended in 1915. This world's fair was intended to celebrate the completion of the Panama Canal, but it also gave San Franciscans a way to celebrate their city's recovery from the 1906 earthquake.

dunes, propelled especially by an internal spark tenderly kept alive and glowing by my father."

When the exposition ended on December 4, 1915, Ansel returned to the Wilkins School, a traditional school with a tireless teacher who read Ansel his lessons out loud and gave him all As. Ansel graduated from the eighth grade and his formal education officially ended. He never attended high school or college. This non-traditional, early education set the stage for a non-traditional life.

Music vs. Mountains

As is the case with many young people, it wasn't immediately clear to young Ansel Adams what he would do with his life. At age 12 he discovered a love and talent for the piano. At age 14, he was smitten by the sights and sounds of Yosemite. For much of his teenage and young adult life, these two passions blossomed independently of each other. Ansel devoted himself to music during his winters in San Francisco, but became enthralled with photography during his summers living in Yosemite.

For a very long time, Ansel could not decide what to be: a pianist or a photographer. At the time, photography was not considered a real career, and his mother was a huge supporter of the piano. Not until he was almost 20 years old did his two passions converge with an unexpected result, and he finally made his choice. The music vs. mountains debate was professionally put to rest.

LOVE OF MUSIC

The Adams family always had a piano at home. In 1914, when Ansel was 12 years old, his father heard him picking at notes on the keys and decided that Ansel had some real talent. Some sources say Ansel had a somewhat photographic memory and that he quickly taught himself to read music and play the piano with ease. Other sources simply say that Charles Adams heard young Ansel playing and promptly hired him a piano teacher to nurture the boy's musical interest.

Ansel's first piano teacher, Miss Marie Butler, became a powerful force in Ansel's musical pursuits. The no-nonsense, practice-makes-perfect Butler—together with the music—brought a discipline and purpose to Ansel's life that hadn't been there before. In the piano, Ansel also found a new, socially acceptable way to calm his active mind. "The change from a hyperactive Sloppy Joe was not over-night," Adams later wrote in his autobiography, "but was sufficiently abrupt to make some startled people ask 'What happened?'" Young Ansel threw himself into music with force and enthusiasm, often practicing for many hours each day.

Over time, Butler taught Ansel techniques that allowed him to express himself with sound. The music became a means for Ansel to vocalize his emotions. He stuck with his piano lessons in a very serious way. As a teenager, Ansel moved on to other, more senior instructors. By 1923, at age 21, he was a budding professional pianist in need of a more professional instrument to fine-tune his skills. Again, his father stepped in.

In 1925 Charles helped Ansel purchase a $6,700 Mason and Hamlin grand piano (at that time, a small car cost only about $500). Ansel kept the piano, always remembered as a very fine instrument, until his death in 1984. He started practicing on the new piano for six or more hours a day and began teaching piano lessons (partly to help pay off the instrument). He was known to his friends and family as a pianist, but his small hands and blossoming passion for photography soon put an end to any serious pursuit of a career as a concert pianist.

In time, Ansel applied what he learned about expressing his emotions musically to his photography. "I am convinced that expla-nation of emotion in art is accomplished only in the medium in which it is created," Ansel wrote in his autobiography. "This came to me powerfully years later when I came to photography."

LOVE OF YOSEMITE

Just two years after his first piano lesson, Ansel made his first visit to Yosemite. His memories of that first trip are consistently moving. In multiple interviews, articles, films, and writings, he noted that Yosemite made an immediate impact on his life. "I knew my destiny when I first experienced Yosemite," he wrote in his 1985 autobiography.

As Ansel's passion for Yosemite grew and developed, so did his interest in photography. During the summer of 1916 in Yosemite, Ansel likely took more than 50 photographs with his first camera, the Kodak Box Brownie. (There is no exact photographic record of that first visit.)

In 1917, Ansel met two influential new photography teachers. That winter he started working at Frank Dittiman's photo-finishing business down the street from his home in San Francisco. There, the largely self-taught Ansel learned to develop and process photographic negatives well enough to do the work part time. That summer, he also met Francis Holman at Yosemite—a man he called Uncle Frank—who took him on long hikes through the Yosemite wilderness. From then on, winters were spent perfecting his darkroom techniques and developing and printing photographs. Summers were spent at Yosemite gathering new photographic negatives.

GOING DEEPER INTO YOSEMITE

Francis Holman became Ansel's unofficial guide to the Yosemite wilderness. Though Ansel knew little about the man, he did know that Holman had graduated from the Massachusetts Institute of Technology in 1877, worked as a mining engineer in South America for many years, collected birds in Yosemite for the San Francisco Academy of Sciences, and was a skilled camper and fisherman. After their first meeting in Yosemite in 1917, Holman served as Ansel's personal wilderness mentor for many years.

The two became real friends. Together they went on many overnight trips during which Ansel learned to camp, cook, and navigate his way through the summer. With wilderness-savvy Uncle Frank, Ansel's outdoor adventures became more and more intense. In a

Mt. Starr King, shown here in a view from Glacier Point Road in Yosemite, was an early hiking destination of Ansel Adams.

letter to his mother in May 1918, published in 1988 in *Ansel Adams: Letters and Images: 1916–1984,* Ansel wrote:

> I started out at 5 o'clock this morning with Mr. Holman for Mt. Starr King. There is no trail and it is one of the hardest trips I have ever taken—perfectly safe however . . . We got to the base of the peak after a long tramp through big snow fields and began to look for a place to start the ascent . . . It was almost perpendicular for 500 feet [152.4 meters] and appeared so dangerous that I resolved to turn back. Mr. Holman cut steps in the snow and reached the top, I guess the first man to ever do so as it has been considered un-climbable.

Ansel and Uncle Frank went on many exploratory trips through Yosemite. By 1920, Ansel had become an educated authority on the

Yosemite Valley wilderness. During this summer he bought a mule to help him carry his increasing load of photographic equipment on his overnight wilderness trips. He and Uncle Frank planned their first journey into the High Sierra, the mountain ridges found roughly between 8,000 to 14,000 feet (2,438 to 4,267 m) of elevation. Adams later remembered his first trip into the High Sierra as his introduction to real wilderness, and he soon gained enough confidence and experience to begin exploring the land solo.

Ansel started hiking alone, and he often hiked alone for days, ignorant to any surrounding dangers such as bears or his dwindling

Ansel Adams, pictured here circa 1920, started his photography work by making an image diary of the mountains he visited.

food supplies. He treasured his solitary time outdoors and the opportunities this gave him to take more photographs. "The snapshots that I made on my early Yosemite excursions were studied at other times of the year with unflagging interest," Adams recalled in his autobiography. "My purpose, during those first years of photography, was to make a visual diary of my mountain trips." At this point in Ansel's life, his photographs were not so much art as they were a way for him to share his experiences with others and document what he saw. For the moment, Ansel had no real intention of making photography his career.

To fund his growing photography hobby and his summer excursions in Yosemite, Ansel again followed in the footsteps of his Uncle Frank, taking over a job at Yosemite that his wilderness mentor had held for many years.

THE LECONTE MEMORIAL LODGE

For many years, Francis Holman worked as the custodian for the LeConte Memorial Lodge, a simple stone cottage located in Curry Village in the Yosemite Valley, the last-stop visitor center for anyone headed into the wilderness. The custodian would care for the building and answer visitors' questions in the busy summer months. It was a perfect job for young Ansel.

When Ansel learned that the lodge was in need of a new custodian in the summer of 1919, he quickly applied and was hired. He worked as the lodge custodian in the summers from 1920 to 1924. His job as custodian cemented a lifelong relationship with the Sierra Club, the owners of the lodge.

The LeConte Memorial Lodge was built in 1903 by the Sierra Club, a San Francisco-based environmental organization founded by writer and conservationist John Muir. The lodge was meant to serve as a library and retreat for the club's members. Since its construction, the lodge has also served as the base camp for Sierra Club Outings—trips into the wilderness and the High Sierra led by experienced guides.

A BRIEF INTRODUCTION TO THE SIERRA CLUB

The Sierra Club is the oldest environmental organization in the United States. It was founded by conservationist and writer John Muir (1838–1914) in May 1892 in San Francisco. Its original goal was to help preserve and protect California's High Sierra, also known as the Sierra Nevada, a name meaning "snowy mountain range." The High Sierra is a ridge of mountains stretching 400 miles (650 km) north to south through the state of California. Since the club's creation, it has served as the unofficial guardian and guide for Yosemite National Park.

As a guardian of the Yosemite Valley, the Sierra Club has done many different things. Muir wrote many popular articles and books about the High Sierra that helped inspire President Franklin D. Roosevelt to federally preserve the area as a national park. Since then, the club has worked to maintain trails, build huts and lodges, and preserve the wilderness areas in and around Yosemite. One of

Today, the LeConte Memorial Lodge still stands in Curry Village, but its management and role in the park have changed. The National Park Service built a larger facility in Yosemite Village to serve as the main headquarters and visitor's center. The National Park Service now owns the LeConte Memorial Lodge, but the Sierra Club operates it as a Yosemite library, museum, and lecture hall.

As the lodge custodian employed by the Sierra Club, Ansel began leading one club Outing per week into the Yosemite Valley and its rims. The routine was always the same: Ansel would meet his group of about eight people for breakfast and they would talk about where they were headed. Then they would spend the day touring the valley, with Ansel taking pictures all along the way.

their goals is to preserve the wildness of Yosemite while making it accessible to the public.

To do this, the Sierra Club leads dozens of guided trips, called Outings, into Yosemite and other wilderness areas in the United States and around the world. The Sierra Club began its Outings program unofficially in 1901 when Sierra Club secretary William Colby led a group of people into the Yosemite Valley. These early Outings were huge expeditions that sometimes involved 100 people. Many of the first ascents of mountains in the High Sierra were made by people on Sierra Club Outings, and early Outings leaders were pioneers of modern rock climbing techniques. Ansel Adams got his own start with the Sierra Club leading one of these early Outings in Yosemite.

Today, the Sierra Club still leads Outings, and the program has grown significantly. Multiple small and large groups take guided trips throughout the nation and the world. The Sierra Club offers more than 350 Outings options on its Web site at http://www. sierraclub.org/outings.

By then, Ansel was likely mastering his fourth camera—an early, single-lens reflex (SLR) camera called a Graflex. SLR cameras make it possible for the photographer to look directly through the camera's lens at the object being photographed. This technology is widely used in cameras today. Ansel began with the simple Kodak Box Brownie in 1916, used a glass-plate camera of an unknown brand in 1917, and switched to a Kodak pocket camera in 1918 and 1919. When he started using the Graflex, it seems he began to pay more attention to the composition and feel of his photographs.

In a long letter to his father during that first summer as lodge custodian, there is little mention of his Sierra Club duties or the many visitors he met. Instead, Ansel tries to explain his photographic pursuits to his father and sends him sample photographs to prove his point. One such photograph, *Diamond Cascade,* taken in 1920, is offered as an example of his early success. "I want you to see what I am trying to do in pictorial photography," Ansel wrote in a letter to his father. "It is the representation of material things in the abstract or purely imaginative way. I feel quite happy over this picture, to my mind it is the most satisfactory composition I have yet done."

VIRGINIA ROSE BEST ADAMS (1904–2000)

Virginia Rose Best was the only daughter of Harry and Ann Best. She grew up in Yosemite, helping run her parents' small gift shop, climbing mountains, and studying to be a classical singer. She married Ansel Adams in 1928 and began juggling her varied roles as mother, wife, and conservationist.

Virginia was a longtime member of the Sierra Club. She and Ansel shared a desire to conserve Yosemite and keep it from being over-commercialized. Virginia served on the Sierra Club's board of directors from 1931 to 1933, when the couple's first child was born.

Virginia and Ansel had two children: Michael, born in 1933, and Anne, born in 1935. For both births, Ansel was away taking pictures. When Virginia's father died in 1936, she inherited Best's Studio, a small gift shop located in Yosemite. Because Ansel traveled often for his work, Virginia stayed home to care for the children, their home, and the gift shop. By all counts, those who knew her remembered her as the rock that made Ansel's career possible. "She was sort of the unsung hero," says Michael Adams in the PBS film *Ansel Adams.* "My mom had the business in Yosemite . . . [and that] enabled them to live and Ansel to have more time to do the

Diamond Cascade is an example of Ansel's experimentation with different types of photographic styles. Instead of trying to take a picture of a waterfall that looked like a waterfall, Ansel was going for a more abstract image, one in which the waterfall no longer looked like a waterfall, but instead evoked other shapes and textures. Ansel's pursuit of abstract, pictorial photography was actually quite short, and he soon began taking more realistic pictures. At the same time, his letters and photographs from this period arguably reveal

[creative work]. Commercial jobs were very important but her support financially allowed him to do a lot of things that he might not otherwise have been doing."

At the same time, Virginia was very modest about her own talents. She was an aspiring classical singer, something Adams always supported her in, at least verbally. She was quite an accomplished hiker of her time, too, and was the first person to ascend two peaks in Sequoia National Park in California. This was at a time when women didn't often pursue physical goals. She published numerous books, including a guidebook to Yosemite and a popular children's book, *Michael and Anne in Yosemite Valley* (1941).

Later in life, Virginia, Ansel, and three friends began a publishing company called Five Associates, which created quality postcards and note cards made from Adams's photographs. Virginia eventually turned Five Associates over to her daughter, Anne, who renamed the business Museum Graphics. The company still operates today.

After Ansel Adams died in 1988, Virginia continued to run Best's Studio at Yosemite. In 1971, the studio was renamed the Ansel Adams Gallery and Virginia managed it until her death at age 96. Staffers say her powerful presence there is remembered daily.

that young Ansel was thinking less and less about the piano, and more and more about photography as a serious form of art.

In 1922, the *Sierra Club Bulletin* published some of Ansel's photographs of Yosemite. They were the first published photographs of his career. Although he still clung to his love of music, it seemed that his love for the mountains had started to take over his professional pursuits.

ANSEL ADAMS MEETS VIRGINIA

During the summer of 1921, when Adams was 19 years old and working as the lodge custodian, he decided to find a piano at Yosemite that he could use to practice his music. If he was really going to become a concert pianist, he thought, he could not afford to take a three-month break every summer.

The only piano Adams could locate was at Best's Studio, a Yosemite gift shop that sold woodcarvings, paintings, and books. The small shop was owned and operated by Harry Best. His 17-year-old daughter, Virginia, kept house and made meals for her father after her mother died in 1920. Harry generously let Adams use his piano, and Adams soon came to visit Virginia as much as he did the piano. Their friendship slowly grew, and Ansel wrote to his father about his first love in July 1922. As published in Adams's autobiography, the letter explained:

> I have met someone, whom I have grown very fond of indeed. A very lovely character—one whose affection is a privilege to possess . . . Pa, I have been hit very hard, and I make no pretense of denying it—for I am proud of it . . . The world seems fuller, more beautiful—there is something in it now that was not there before, something I did not dream would come so soon. I am beginning to realize what real life is—life of the loftiest kind.

Adams and Virginia dated seriously for six years before they were finally married in 1928. The courtship was not smooth, however, with Adams still splitting his time between San Francisco and Yosemite, and still undecided career-wise between the music and the mountains. Many of his thoughts of the time are preserved in the many dozens of letters the two wrote to each other during this period.

By 1923, for example, Adams was still intent on a career as a concert pianist but wrote to Virginia about his eagerness to return to her and the mountains. His letters from September of this year explained his determination to devote his time to his music. "I will continue my photographic work as a means of incidental income until I find my music is filling my time," he wrote, later to be published in *Letters and Images,* 1988. "Thereafter the photography will become a hobby only. I cannot let anything interfere with my music, which is my life's work. I have definitely made up my mind about photography."

By 1925, still intent on not letting anything interfere with his music, Adams broke up with Virginia and returned to San Francisco to become a musician. Without the distraction of Virginia and the mountains of Yosemite, he figured, he would be free to pursue his career as a pianist. Virginia was more upset than she let Adams see, and stayed safely hidden in her Yosemite home.

During the breakup, Adams pursued many girlfriends but had no serious relationships. It didn't take long before he got tired of his life as a budding professional musician. In 1927, he finally decided to abandon his musical career for good and turned back to the mountains, to photography, and to Virginia.

Adams went to Yosemite to celebrate the New Year with Virginia in 1928, and then he formally proposed to her. They were married three days later, on January 2, 1928, at Best's Studio. Adams's parents, Harry Best, and a few friends were present for the occasion. With Adams's commitment to marriage, it seems, came his commitment to the pursuit of photography as an art and as a career.

Photography
Takes Root

When Ansel Adams finally decided to devote his time and talent to photography, he got mixed reactions from his family. Virginia was supportive, always the believer at his side. His mother and Aunt Mary felt otherwise. "Do not give up the piano! The camera cannot express the human soul!" he remembers being scolded by them. To this he replied, "Perhaps the camera cannot, but the photographer can."

At the time, photography was not considered an art. Pictures were practical. Pictures were sold as postcards and in cheap gift shops. Yet photographs were not of the same quality and value as paintings, sculptures, or music. Adams helped change this perception. He developed his own style of photography and technical guidelines for taking photographs, which he shared with thousands of students and interested people during his lifetime.

Almost by accident, the photographs of the wild lands he loved in Yosemite and throughout the United States moved others to love those lands as well. They moved people who hadn't even been to Yosemite or thought about streams, mountains, animals, or the value of pure wilderness areas. When other people saw Adams's photographs, they often started thinking about conserving the beauty of the wild places shown to them in Adams's art.

Over time, as more and more people began to see Adams's photographs, the photographs themselves became serious conservation tools. It all started in the late 1920s, when Adams finally turned his attention to photography as art, and as his career.

EARLY PHOTOGRAPHY

When Adams began thinking seriously about photography as a career in the 1920s, there was no such thing as a photographer who was considered an artist. Artists were people who painted, sculpted, drew, or created other things with their hands. Photographers were people who recorded historical scenes and people so that they could be remembered, archived, or printed in descriptive textbooks. Photography was not yet accepted as an art form. It took a long time to get there.

From about 1885 to the early 1900s, pictorial photographers labored to make photography artistic. The goal was to take photographs that looked like more traditional art—like paintings or drawings of that time. Photographers used all sorts of tools to do this, including using very soft focus lenses to make fuzzy edges on images, special filters to change the shades of color in a photograph, and manipulation in the darkroom when photographs were printed.

When Adams came along as a professional photographer in the mid 1920s, the popularity of pictorial photography was fading. Adams himself hated these attempts to recreate other forms of art in photographs. At the same time, he had experimented with more abstract photography (such as *Diamond Cascade* in 1920), and in the end wasn't thrilled with those results either. Adams favored photographs that accurately represented their subjects—later called straight photography—but somehow possessed some emotional impact as well.

Adams became determined to make artistic photographs; he just hadn't mastered his art yet. "I want to establish a reputation for artistic work," he wrote in a letter to Virginia in 1923, later published in the 1988 book *Letters and Images 1916–1984.* "My photographs will always be purely photographs—not for coloring, not for reproduction in books . . . I want my work to reach really high standards of art." With this attitude, he continued taking photographs and developing prints, collecting them in boxes and showing them to fellow artists and collectors. Then, in 1927, everything changed.

A SMALL SUCCESS

In the spring of 1926, Adams went to a party at a friend's house in San Francisco and took along a box of his photographs. The friend introduced Adams to a man named Albert Bender, saying, "Here's Ansel Adams. He plays pretty good piano and takes damn good photographs," according to Adams's autobiography. Bender, it turned out, was a very rich man always on the lookout for struggling young artists.

Bender slowly inspected Adams's photographs at the party that evening and asked Adams to meet him at his office the next day. At that meeting, Bender immediately suggested Adams gather a collection of mountain photographs and together they would publish them in a professional portfolio. Adams excitedly agreed.

In the following months, Adams made 18 prints of his best mountain photographs for the portfolio. Bender paid for the printing and publishing of 100 portfolios containing these prints, entitled *Parmelian Prints of the High Sierras.* He also started contacting his upper-class, art-collecting friends to buy them for $50 each. At the time, the publisher insisted on using the word *print* in the portfolio title instead of *photograph* because photography was still not yet considered a legitimate art form. Bender bought 20 portfolios for his own collection and the remaining portfolios sold out before the end of 1927. Adams received his first significant paycheck for his photography work.

Bender's encouragement and financial support helped make Adams aware, for the first time, that photography could be a real,

ALBERT MAURICE BENDER (1866–1941)

Albert Bender was a huge patron of the arts in the 1920s and 1930s in San Francisco, providing financial assistance to artists, writers, and museums. He was a very wealthy man, but he never married or had close family, so much of his time and wealth went straight to the arts that he loved.

Bender immigrated to San Francisco from Germany in 1881 when he was 15 years old and began working in his uncle's insurance business. He was smart and worked well, and eventually Bender began his own, very successful insurance firm. Because he loved literature and art, he started collecting rare books and modern works of art, particularly from San Francisco, China, and Japan. He worked hard to share these collections and his wealth with the world.

In 1912, for example, Bender helped create the nonprofit organization Book Club of California, still in action today, which helps promote the collection, understanding, and appreciation of fine books. Throughout the early 1900s, he donated significant pieces of art to what are now the Fine Arts Museum of San Francisco and the San Francisco Museum of Modern Art.

At the same time, Bender was widely known for supporting and helping launch the careers of young, struggling artists such as Ansel Adams. He used his time, his connections, and his money to help get the works of a new artist seen and recognized.

Yet, to Adams, Bender was more than just a rich patron. Adams helped care for Bender until his peaceful death in 1941. In his autobiography, Adams describes Bender as an extraordinary person and a true philanthropist—often helping not only artists, but also janitors, mailmen, and waitresses whom he met and took a liking to throughout his life: "His example of nobility and generosity bore fruit in many orchards of the human spirit," Adams wrote in his autobiography.

paying career. And the two soon became real friends. Bender became Adams's contact to a new world of creative—and often wealthy—people. He would often call Adams and take him on unplanned excursions to meet new people and see new works of art in museums and homes around San Francisco. Unless Adams was under a strict deadline, he always went wherever Bender suggested they go. Because Bender did not drive, Adams would chauffer the pair around in Bender's own car.

The experience helped cement photography as an art in Adams's own mind, and he soon became excited about his newly discovered style. As he wrote to Virginia in April 1927:

> I have been so very busy and I have so many new ideas. I feel now I
> am more or less settled on something definite . . . My photographs
> have now reached a stage when they are worthy of the world's criti-
> cal examination. I have suddenly come upon a new style which I
> believe will place my work equal to anything of its kind.

This new style soon became known as "straight photography," an attempt to depict a scene realistically and objectively, and Adams was not alone in his passion for it. He didn't want to make a photograph that looked like a painting. He wanted to make a photograph that captured the things he saw in nature.

The publication of his first portfolio in 1927 and his growing friendship with Albert Bender set the stage for Adams's national success as an artistic photographer. With that came a career as an effective conservationist.

ARTISTIC SUCCESS

With the success of Adams's first portfolio came his first, more personal, artistic breakthrough that stayed with him for the remainder of his life. One day in 1927, Adams climbed a mountain in Yosemite with the intent of photographing the face of Half Dome. He shot many photos that day, but it was only when he was down to his

Monolith, the Face of Half Dome is considered by many experts to be one of Ansel Adams's most amazing images. Here, Adams poses in front of the photograph as it hung in his California home in December 1980.

last picture of the day that he visualized what he really wanted the image to look like and how he would make that happen. As Adams described to the Wilderness Society in 1980:

> . . . that was the first time I realized how the print was going to look—what I now call visualization—and was actually thinking about the emotional effect of the image . . . I began to visualize the black rock and deep sky. I really wanted to give it a monumental, dark quality. So I used the last plate [photograph] I had with a No. 29-F red filter . . . and got this exciting picture.

The picture he refers to here, *Monolith, the Face of Half Dome,* is still regarded by experts as one of Adams's most compelling and memorable photographs. Adams knew the photograph was something special when he took it that day in 1927. As he told the Wilderness Society, he had visualized the image before it was even printed, a technique he later elaborated on and taught to others extensively.

Visualization—sometimes called pre-visualization—is an approach to photography with two basic steps: one artistic and one technical. First, Adams insisted that a photographer (himself included) must be able to picture the final print of an image before snapping the shutter of the camera. This includes understanding not only the subjects of the photograph, but also the difference between the light and dark pieces of the photograph, known as the contrast. Picturing the photograph in one's mind in this way is the artistic part of the process, according to Adams.

Second, Adams said, the photographer must take the technical steps needed to create that visualized image with the camera. Only with the correct combination of light and lens can a visualized print actually be produced. Over time, Adams became an expert at visualizing images in his mind, and then using his technical knowledge to produce the prints he wanted.

Adams, at this point, had a technique he could use to create the straight photography images of the wild places he treasured. And he wasn't the only one to treasure such images.

BIG SUCCESSES

Armed with this new technique and more confidence in his own approach to photography, Adams was met with a string of big successes. He began journeying to New Mexico and meeting with other now-famous and influential artists. Adams became a leader of the national movement in straight photography, and he had the first large exhibition of his own work in New York City. With these successes and milestones, Adams's professional photography career took off.

Trips to New Mexico

In 1927, Adams visited New Mexico for the first time and fell in love with the lights and sights of the Southwest. Bender accompanied Adams on this first trip, and the two met and visited other writers and artists living in Santa Fe, including writer Mary Austin and artist Georgia O'Keeffe.

While on this trip, Bender and Adams decided to make another portfolio of photographs of the Southwest. Adams soon got to work. The portfolio, *Taos Pueblo,* was published in 1930 and contained a collection of 12 of Adams's New Mexico photographs. Only 108 copies of the portfolio were printed and they quickly sold out. It is now considered a rare collector's book and sells for about $3,000.

In time, Adams and Virginia made many friends in New Mexico and returned there repeatedly throughout his photography career for inspiration and relaxation. Many of Adams's most famous photographs were taken on these trips.

f/64

In 1932, Adams was at a party of fellow artists, excitedly explaining his newfound passion for straight photography. He found he was not at all alone. Adams and six other photographers at the party agreed then and there to form a group opposed to the old-fashioned rules of pictorial photography, and become outspoken supporters of straight photography.

The group called itself f/64, which is the setting on a camera lens that brings a sharp focus to the final image. The seven of them set out to present frequent shows of straight photography. In November

Church, Taos Pueblo, photographed by Adams in 1942, is one of the many images he took during his visits to New Mexico.

1932, f/64 opened its first straight photography exhibition at the M.H. de Young Memorial Museum in San Francisco, showing photographs by Adams and the other six founding members of the group.

By 1935, some members of f/64 had moved away from San Francisco and many artists were feeling the impact of the Great Depression, a time when many people nationwide lost jobs and money. As a result, f/64 dissolved, but the straight photography that the small group helped make reputable lives on.

Adams's First National Exhibition

In 1932, Harry Best gave Adams and Virginia $1,000 to take a vacation to New York City. Virginia had recently learned she was pregnant with her first baby, and the couple wanted to travel before starting a family. In 1933, they boarded the train in San Francisco headed for the East Coast.

In New York, Adams went to meet Alfred Stieglitz, a photographer and owner of An American Place, a well-known art gallery in the city. Their first meeting was brisk as Adams had arrived at Stieglitz's gallery unannounced and ready to show off his photographs. But when Stieglitz examined Adams's work carefully and quietly at their second meeting, he simply told Adams that he was welcome to come see him anytime. Adams returned to Stieglitz's gallery annually for the next four years to show the art icon his photographs.

Finally, something happened at one of these meetings. In January 1936 Stieglitz decided Adams—now a father of two and still developing as a photographer—was ready for his own art show at An American Place. It was the biggest venue for artistic photographers of that time. Adams worked for the next eight months to prepare his photographs for the exhibition, the first nationally recognized, one-man show of his career. The show was considered a success among artists and art critics.

In a letter to Stieglitz after the show closed, as quoted in Adams's autobiography, Adams wrote, "My work has become new and exciting to me as never before . . . I can see only one thing to do—make the photography as clean, as decisive, and as honest as possible." Arguably, that is just what Adams did.

THE ACCIDENTAL CONSERVATIONIST EMERGES

At the same time as Adams's photography career was taking off, he was quietly gaining a foothold in the budding conservation

ALFRED STIEGLITZ (1864–1946)

Alfred Stieglitz was an influential photographer and the owner of An American Place, a well-known art gallery in New York City. He was born in Hoboken, New Jersey, where he lived until 1881 when his father sold his company and moved the family to southwest Germany.

While taking a chemistry class in Germany in 1882, Stieglitz met a chemist working on the then-evolving process of chemical photography. Stieglitz reportedly found photography both academically challenging and a good outlet for his artistic mind. He was hooked.

American photographer and art promoter Alfred Stieglitz helped popularize photography as an art form. Through his New York art galleries, he introduced many avant-garde artists to American audiences. He was married to painter Georgia O'Keeffe.

Stieglitz lived and traveled around Europe, taking photographs during the next ten years. By 1890 he considered himself an artist with

movement. By now Adams and his family had two homes: one they built next to Charles and Olive in San Francisco, and one in Yosemite, where Virginia continued to run her father's store and raise their two children, Michael and Anne. While living in

a camera and refused to work in a field other than photography. He moved back to New York and married.

There he began writing for early photography magazines and publishing his photographs, quickly developing a name for himself. In 1896, he became vice president of the Camera Club of New York, with the goal of making photography as artistic and respected in the United States as it was in Europe. He also began putting together exhibitions of other artists' work and showing them in his own small gallery.

In 1917 Stieglitz met painter Georgia O'Keeffe, divorced his first wife, and eventually married O'Keeffe. He began exhibiting her paintings, and continued to exhibit the work of other artists. Stieglitz was reportedly a perfectionist in the gallery, and to hold an exhibition there was considered an artistic triumph. In 1936, Stieglitz gave Ansel Adams his first one-man photography show in New York City.

For Adams, Stieglitz would not only expose his photography to a national audience of critics and collectors, but he would also give him some artistic direction. "Rather than say Stieglitz influenced me in my work," Adams wrote in his autobiography, "I would say that he revealed me to myself . . . He was an enigma, a crank, an artist, a genius, an editor, a publisher, a dealer in art, a tastemaker, an influence. He believed that the artist has a right to work with dignity, thinking and doing as he desires." Some say Stieglitz was the most influential figure in visual arts in the United States during his lifetime. He certainly influenced Ansel Adams.

Yosemite, the Sierra Club soon became an important part of their lives.

In 1927, Adams and Virginia traveled with the Sierra Club to Sequoia National Park, about 140 miles (222 km) from Yosemite. In 1928, 1929, 1930, and 1932, Adams was the official photographer on the Sierra Club Outings. By 1934 he was elected to the board of directors, a position he would hold for the next 37 years.

As Adams's photographic talent became more and more clear, he and others began to realize that his photographs could be used as powerful conservation tools. If nothing else, his photographs got people to stop and pay attention to nature.

Creating
Kings Canyon

As a member of the board of directors for the Sierra Club, Ansel Adams began to use all the tools he had—showing his photographs, writing letters, and talking to people—to help the Sierra Club in its mission. The club's mission, as stated on its Web site, is "to explore, enjoy, and protect the wild places of the earth."

The club's priority issue in the 1930s was to protect an area southeast of Yosemite known as Kings Canyon. It was a place Adams had hiked and photographed countless times by this point in his life. When he joined the Sierra Club in 1936, Adams immediately started working with the club to convince lawmakers and senators to officially protect Kings Canyon by making it a national park. Eventually, the process to protect Kings Canyon became Adams's first real taste of success in conservation.

Adams photographed parts of Kings River Canyon for a National Park Service project. This image, noted by Adams as "Middle Fork at Kings River from South Fork of Cartridge Creek," was taken in February 1936.

PHOTOGRAPHY AS A CONSERVATION TOOL

It's not exactly clear when Adams first realized that his photography could be an effective tool to convince lawmakers to protect wild places by showing them the unique beauty of the land. He figured this out quickly in his work with Kings Canyon. One of Adams's photography books was a major tool in the fight for the canyon. Sometime in the early 1930s, Adams was asked by Walter Starr, a fellow Sierra Club member, to put together a book of Sierra photographs in honor of his son, Peter, who had died in a mountaineering accident in Yosemite in 1933. Starr was familiar with Adams's artistic work and offered to fund the production of the books only if they were printed in the highest quality possible. Adams agreed. In 1938, just 500 copies of the book, *Sierra Nevada: The John Muir Trail,* were published. The book became both an artistic success and a powerful conservation tool.

Artistically, the book received rave reviews. Adams sent a copy of *Sierra Nevada* to Alfred Stieglitz, the icon of artistic photography at the time, and received a glowing letter of thanks in return. "You have literally taken my breath away," Stieglitz wrote in 1938. "What perfect photography . . . I am glad to have lived to see this happen. And here in America. All American. I am elated."

At the same time, *Sierra Nevada* became a powerful conservation tool. Adams sent copies of the book to influential lawmakers in Washington, D.C., in an effort to turn their attention to protecting Kings Canyon from the encroaching developers hoping to commercialize Yosemite Valley. Soon, the Sierra Club sent Adams to Washington to present more photographs of the region and to help convince lawmakers that the area deserved protection.

Adams was happy to present his photographs and talk about them at length, but he insisted throughout his life that he never took a photograph solely for conservation purposes. For Adams, his photographs were art and nothing more. Yet if they happened to convince others that wild places were beautiful and worth protecting, then he was happy.

Many of the photographs of the Kings Canyon region that Adams took to Washington in 1936 had been shot decades earlier, but they became these unintended conservation tools. The experience was Adams's introduction to Washington, D.C., and the politics of conservation. It was perhaps the first time he realized that his photographs could be so influential.

Adams Goes to Washington

The Sierra Club was already aware—perhaps more than Adams himself—of the power of photography in lobbying lawmakers to protect wild places. Photographs of Yosemite taken by Carleton Watkins, a photographer who first went to California in search of gold and fortune, had helped persuade the government to set aside the Yosemite Valley for protection in 1864. Photographs of Yellowstone taken by William Henry Jackson, a painter and photographer, had helped create the first national park in 1872.

In 1936, the Sierra Club asked Adams to represent the club at a parks conference in Washington, D.C. They wanted him to use his

President Franklin D. Roosevelt (*left*) poses with his cabinet in March 1933. Secretary of the Interior Harold L. Ickes is the second man on his right. Ickes fought to establish Kings Canyon National Park by using Adams's photos to encourage members of the U.S. Congress to send the bill to President Roosevelt in 1940.

photographs of the Kings Canyon region to present the club's ideas for protection of that area. Adams took many of his photographs to senators and lawmakers to make the case for the club. He spoke confidently and unabashedly about the glory of the region, and he did get some people to pay attention. The land was not protected that year, but Adams had started the ball rolling. In coming years, Adams and the Sierra Club continued to use his photographs for conservation purposes.

In 1938 Adams sent a copy of his newly published book, *Sierra Nevada: The John Muir Trail,* to Secretary of the Interior Harold L. Ickes, the man who oversaw the National Park Service. Ickes reportedly took the book over to President Franklin D. Roosevelt and used it to persuade him to support the Kings Canyon National Park idea. Ickes wrote to Adams in January 1939:

> My dear Mr. Adams:
>
> I am enthusiastic about the book—*The John Muir Trail*—which you were so generous to send me. The pictures are extraordinarily fine and impressive. I hope that before this session of Congress adjourns the John Muir National Park in the Kings Canyon area will be a legal fact. Then we can be sure that your descendants and mine will be able to take as beautiful pictures as you have taken—that is, provided they have your skill and artistry.
>
> > Sincerely yours,
> > Harold L. Ickes
> > Secretary of the Interior

Roosevelt wanted to keep Ickes's copy of the book, so Adams was asked to send another copy for the secretary. Clearly, Adams's photographs had made a great impression on the man in charge of preserving wild lands.

WRITING AS A CONSERVATION TOOL

When Adams's 1936 trip to Washington didn't immediately produce protection for the Kings Canyon area, he began writing letters to

HAROLD LECLAIR ICKES (1874–1952)

Harold Ickes was born in Pennsylvania but moved to Chicago at age 16 when his mother died. He was elected class president in high school, graduated from the University of Chicago, and started working as a newspaper reporter and writer. In 1907, he went back to school and got a law degree from the University of Chicago. But instead of practicing law, Ickes turned his attention to politics.

Ickes was active in Chicago politics until 1933, when a friend recommended him to President Franklin D. Roosevelt as a middle-of-the-road Republican for his cabinet. Ickes served as secretary of the interior for 13 years, from 1933 to 1946, the longest time that anyone has held that office in history. He was a member of Roosevelt's cabinet for the entire presidency.

During his tenure as secretary, Ickes became known for many things: He was a strong supporter of civil rights and civil liberties, a proponent of desegregating the national parks, and he greatly opposed corruption of any sort. Over time, he earned the nickname "Honest Harold."

lawmakers, politicians, editors, and newspapers—anyone who would listen. Sierra Club colleagues remember Adams sitting at his typewriter, pounding out letter after letter in support of Sierra Club causes during his 37-year tenure with the board. Some say Adams wrote well over 5,000 letters as a member of the Sierra Club alone, but there is no complete record of his club-related writings—just tidbits here and there.

Adams's autobiography contains a spattering of his writings for the *Sierra Club Bulletin,* the club's main publication for its members. Many of these writings simply express Adams's love of

As much as he is remembered for his work with national parks, he is best remembered as the manager of the Public Works Administration, the agency established during the Great Depression to create jobs. In this role, Ickes managed billions of dollars used to construct dams, bridges, and other large-scale public structures.

He was said to be a great fan of Ansel Adams's photographs, even before Adams began lobbying for Kings Canyon National Park on behalf of the Sierra Club. In 1941, one year after the park was created, Ickes hired Adams to make a photographic mural display for the Department of the Interior's office building in Washington, D.C. Ickes wanted a mural that reflected the department's mission: Protect the country's beautiful land and properly manage resources and the people they serve. Because of the outbreak of U.S. involvement in World War II, the project was never finished, but some of Adams's photographs were eventually hung in the office building.

On March 10, 2010, Secretary of the Interior Ken Salazar finally revealed Adams's national park murals on display in the Department of the Interior's main building. The murals are intended to honor both Adams's and Ickes's work.

the mountains or detail his adventures on club Outings. Others were more persuasive, intent on convincing others of the value of beautiful land. Together, the writings convey the enthusiasm and respect for the wilderness that Adams often used when working on conservation issues with the club. The following is a sampling of his writings from the *Bulletin* in 1932, as published in his autobiography in 1985:

"No matter how sophisticated you may be, a large granite mountain cannot be denied—it speaks in silence to the very core of your being."

"A spirit of unearthly beauty moved in the darkness and spoke in terms of song and the frail music of violins. You were aware of the almost mystic peace that came over us all . . ."

"The American mode of appreciation is dominantly theatrical— often oblivious of the subtle beauty in quiet, simple things . . . It is

CHEAT SHEET:
KINGS CANYON NATIONAL PARK

Kings Canyon National Park is a 462,901-acre (187,329-ha) swatch of land just east of Fresno, California. It is about half the size of the state of Rhode Island and is home to two major attractions: the largest remaining natural grove of giant sequoia trees in the world, and one of the deepest canyons in the United States.

About 10 percent of the park protects several groves of giant sequoia trees, a type of redwood tree that grows to an average height of 165 to 280 feet (50 to 85 m) and 18 to 24 feet (6 to 8 m) in diameter. Together with the groves protected in Sequoia National Park, a smaller area that borders Kings Canyon to the south, the park is home to the 30 largest giant sequoias in the world. Each tree is estimated to be between 1,800 and 2,700 years old.

The other 90 percent of Kings Canyon National Park is a deep valley with towering granite mountains. One of these is Mt. Whitney, which at 14,491 feet (4,417 m) is the tallest mountain in the lower 48 United States. Another 11 mountains taller than 14,000 feet (4,267 m) are found in the ridge of the High Sierra contained within the park's boundaries.

The valley through the Kings Canyon granite was cut by a slow-moving glacier about 10 million years ago. This makes it a relatively young range of mountains. A few small glaciers remain in the park, and are the southernmost glaciers in North America.

better to accept the continuous beauty of the things that are, and forget comparisons . . ."

Adams himself admits in his autobiography that he made no attempts to hide or polish his love of nature when writing and lobbying to protect a place on behalf of the Sierra Club. He would write

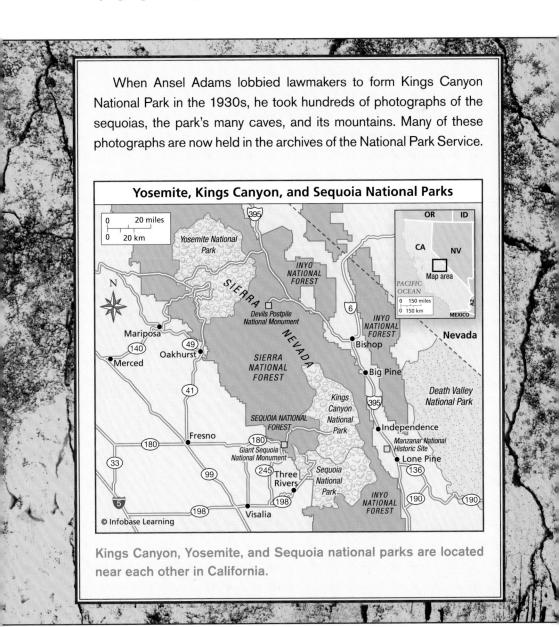

When Ansel Adams lobbied lawmakers to form Kings Canyon National Park in the 1930s, he took hundreds of photographs of the sequoias, the park's many caves, and its mountains. Many of these photographs are now held in the archives of the National Park Service.

Kings Canyon, Yosemite, and Sequoia national parks are located near each other in California.

Adams, shown here in October 1948, was proud that his images of Kings Canyon helped lawmakers see the need to protect the land.

incessantly and passionately until he got what he wanted. In 1940, his conservation efforts paid off in a big way.

KINGS CANYON NATIONAL PARK IS CREATED

After Adams sent copies of *Sierra Nevada: The John Muir Trail* to Secretary of the Interior Ickes and President Roosevelt, both men pressured Congress relentlessly to take action for the region. The

Kings Canyon National Park bill eventually passed in March 1940. Both Adams and administrators agreed that the photographs of the area played a critical role in its conservation. "I realize that a silent but most effective voice in the campaign was your own book," wrote Arno Cammerer, the head of the National Park Service, several years after the bill was passed. Cammerer was also quoted in *Ansel Adams: A Documentary Film*, as saying: "So long as that book is in existence, it will go on justifying the park."

Adams himself believed that his book had been a powerful conservation tool in the fight for Kings Canyon. As he told the Wilderness Society in 1980:

> With what one may call arrogant modesty, I think many of my pictures . . . have an excitement in them which commands more attention than if they were the same scene not composed or adequately printed . . . I think the pictures I had of the Kings Canyon-Sequoia region did have a helpful effect in getting Congress to pass the bill. But no one will ever know whether it was one percent or five percent, or whether it was entirely imaginary.

Even though Kings Canyon became a national park in 1940, its real protection was in doubt for the next 25 years. Many people wanted to build a dam on unprotected lands at the western end of the canyon. If built, the dam could have dried up the lands inside the national park. Instead, the unprotected land was added to the park in 1965 and the canyon was once again preserved.

A TASTE OF CONSERVATION SUCCESS

Adams's efforts to establish Kings Canyon as a protected area gave him a taste of conservation success. He did not stop there. When his beloved Yosemite came under attack soon after the Kings Canyon success, he again used his photographs and letters to preserve the wild place that inspired him the most.

Defending Yosemite

After the creation of Kings Canyon National Park, Adams became more and more involved with the National Park Service and its actions. When a 10-year federal plan to create more roads in the national parks gained speed, for example, Adams became a loud voice of opposition. He wanted to keep the parks wild and let visitors experience them as wild places. Adams was largely against roads, stores, and conveniences, especially when it came to his beloved Yosemite.

He fought loudly to prevent major road and building construction in Yosemite National Park, particularly in an area near Tenaya Lake. The lake, located at an 8,000-foot (2,400 m) elevation, was carved into the granite by glaciers. Again, his many letters to lawmakers to argue on behalf of the wild lands show Adams's devotion to conservation and his passion for the national parks. Yet, unlike his success with Kings Canyon, this time he lost the battle to keep roads out of Yosemite.

In the same decade that he failed (in his mind) to protect Yosemite, he enjoyed ongoing success as a professional photographer. An exhibit of his photographs called "This Is the American Earth" opened at the LeConte Memorial Lodge in Yosemite in 1955 and led to the publication of a book by the same title. It was the first in a series of cof-fee table books put out by the Sierra Club. Despite the defeat at Yosem-ite, Adams's connection to the park and conservation continued—and his two passions of photography and conservation formally converged.

MISSION 66

By the mid 1950s, there were 26 national parks in the United States and more and more people were visiting them. So many people were visiting, in fact, that the existing roads, bathrooms, and other service-oriented buildings weren't quite enough to meet park needs. As a result, in 1955 the director of the National Park Service, Con-rad Wirth, proposed a plan called Mission 66. It took off.

Mission 66 ran from 1956 to 1966 (hence the "66" in the name, the anticipated date of the project's completion) to improve the roads in the national parks and construct new service and education buildings. This included the construction of park visitor centers, the now-common buildings near the entrance of the parks that house offices, park information, maps, food, bathrooms, and educational displays.

Prior to Mission 66, such central visitor centers did not exist. They were intended to make the parks more accessible and under-standable to the public. The new visitor centers, with their accom-panying roads, became instantly recognizable new features of the national parks—for better or worse.

Widely considered to bring some much-needed improvement to the national parks, not everyone agreed with the $1 billion modern-ization effort of Mission 66—especially when it came to blasting a new road through the wilderness of Yosemite. Ansel Adams was one who adamantly disagreed.

PROTECTING YOSEMITE

The Tioga Pass (also called the Tioga Road and California State Route 120) is the highest road through the mountains in the High Sierra of Yosemite National Park, at an elevation of 9,943 feet (3,031 m). It was first built as a small, one-lane road in 1916 and was eventually paved in 1937. With the creation of Mission 66, the road was slated for major expansion.

In order to improve the Tioga Pass road and make the area more accessible to park visitors, the National Park Service planned to dynamite a 3-mile (4.8-km) stretch of granite mountain near Tenaya Lake. Adams, still working with the Sierra Club, thought this was a very destructive and unneeded change. He began to write letters and articles against road development in Tioga Pass and against Mission 66 in general.

Among his many letters from this time is one he wrote to David Brower, then the executive director of the Sierra Club, in 1957. In the letter, Adams urged Brower to be more critical of the growing National Park Service and Mission 66. He thought the club was not taking a strong enough stance on the project. The long letter is typical of Adams's writings on this issue and his growing concern for the direction of the Sierra Club:

> My concern over the relationship of the National Park Service and the Sierra Club and allied organizations is growing, and I cannot, in all honesty, look upon this situation except with the greatest anxiety and pessimism . . . Is it necessary to desecrate the Lake Tenaya area by construction of a road of "highway" standards? . . . How can they justify the destruction of priceless natural beauty for any reason? . . . In the face of the enormous spiritual and inspirational value of the Parks and the wilderness areas—NO bureau, no plan, no established project, no road, no concessionaire, no works of man or any kind has consequential value.

Adams strongly believed in keeping wilderness areas wild. He did not want more roads and visitor facilities. He did not want food stands and bathrooms. He wanted people to experience the parks as wild places. Here, he felt the Sierra Club was not going in the best direction and he began to split away from the group.

In 1958 Adams began writing as an individual—not as a member of the Sierra Club—to high-level lawmakers such as the secretary of the interior (who was ultimately in charge of the national parks) and the director of the National Park Service. In one 1958 letter to these two individuals, as it appears in an article online in the Ansel Adams Gallery, Adams wrote,

> As an individual and not as a director of the Sierra Club, I wish to lodge a most sincere and severe protest against the desecration of Tenaya Lake . . . which is being perpetrated by the ruthless construction of the new Tioga Road for the National Park Service by the Bureau of Public Roads. The catastrophic damage is entirely unnecessary . . . I consider this desecration as an act of disregard of basic conservation principles which approaches criminal negligence on the part of the bureaus concerned. I urgently request you order an immediate cessation of work on the Tioga Road in the Tenaya Lake area until a truly competent group can study the problems and suggest ways and means of accomplishing completion of this project with minimum damage. I have never opposed appropriate improvement of the Tioga Road but in 40 years' experience in national park and wilderness areas I have never witnessed such an insensitive disregard of prime national park values.

Adams felt so strongly about Tioga Pass that he tried to resign from the Sierra Club so that he could protest more vigorously as an individual. Adams wanted to be free to pursue his cause. He kept protesting, but the Sierra Club never fully accepted his resignation.

In the end, Mission 66 was funded and completed the expansion of the Tioga Pass highway. But Adams's protests did make some impact. After his many letters, work on the road was suspended for 12 days and Brower accompanied the National Park Service director to inspect the area. But by this time, much of the damage had already been done. Some small modifications were made in the name of wilderness preservation and work resumed. The Tenaya Lake area was dynamited and the Tioga Pass was rebuilt in 1961.

DAVID ROSS BROWER (1912–2000)

David Brower founded many environmental organizations and was known as a sometimes-controversial environmentalist. He was the first executive director of the Sierra Club (from 1952 to 1969), and served on its board of directors three separate times (from 1941 to 1953; 1983 to 1988; and 1995 to 2000). When he wanted to get something done, Brower did not mess around. His long list of conservation accomplishments includes:

- Campaigned to keep dams out of Dinosaurs National Monument in Utah and the Grand Canyon in Arizona.
- Worked to establish the Wilderness Act of 1964, a law that defined wilderness in the United States and protected 9.1 million acres (3.7 million ha) of federal land.
- Helped establish North Cascades National Park and Redwood National Park in 1968.
- Started the Sierra Club's Exhibit Format Series of influential coffee-table books (including the first by Ansel Adams in 1960).
- Founded the Friends of the Earth (1969), the League of Conservation Voters (1969), and the Earth Island Institute (1982) among other organizations.

Brower's career in conservation began when he came to the Sierra Club. He started editing the *Sierra Club Bulletin* in 1946, the

MAKING ENDS MEET

Adams spent a lot of time on his conservation work during this part of his life, but he received very little—if any—pay for his time. Photography was his main source of income. And by this point in

club's main publication for its members and the one in which Ansel Adams often published his writings and photographs. Brower was very familiar with Adams and his work. "It is hard to tell which has shaped the other more—Ansel Adams or the Sierra Club," Brower told the Wilderness Society in 1980. "What does matter is that the mutuality was important." Illustrating his extreme love of environmentalism, Brower said of Adams's relationship to the wilderness, "That Ansel Adams came to be recognized as one of the great photographers of this century is a tribute to the places that informed him."

David Brower, executive director of the Sierra Club, stands in front of the Grand Canyon in January 1966.

his life Adams had two teenage children and a wife, so making ends meet was not always easy. He wanted to devote his time to artistic photography and conservation, but he had to balance this with more profitable, moneymaking, commercial photography.

Adams therefore took pictures for catalogs, industrial reports, and architects, and shot portraits in order to pay the bills. He set up a photography studio at his home in San Francisco and hung a simple sign outside the door: "Ansel Easton Adams: Photographer." He received paying work, but it wasn't exciting work for him.

On one project, for example, Adams was hired to photograph a loaf of raisin bread. On another he took pictures of unusual buildings in Los Angeles. On yet another he shot portraits of people who worked for a phone company in New York. He became a well-known and well-paid commercial photographer, but his heart was not in it.

THE ZONE SYSTEM OF PHOTOGRAPHY

On occasion, critics have called Ansel Adams a scientist when it comes to shooting and developing photographs, simply because he was so particular about his technique. But Adams always insisted he was not a scientist; he said he was an artist who simply used an exact technique. Eventually, he wrote and taught this technique for taking photographs, known as the Zone System.

Adams's Zone System is complicated. It is intended to teach the basic technical skills needed—such as the proper exposure times and camera apertures used—to create contrast, or different levels of light and dark, in a photograph. Adams knew many of his students could visualize the photograph they wanted, but they did not have the technical camera skills needed to create that photograph. The Zone System was intended to fix that.

Using the Zone System, a photographer first visualizes the image he or she wants to create. Then the image is broken into different zones, or areas, of light and dark. Each zone is assigned

During this time, Adams worked with color photography, producing more than 3,000 color images. But this was largely his commercial, paying work. Almost all of Adams's artistic photography was done with black-and-white film. He and many of his fellow artists thought color photography was much harder to control in the darkroom, and that over time color photographs would fade. So black-and-white images were where Adams concentrated his artistic efforts—when he had the time for his art.

Adams began to apply for fellowships and artistic grants that would allow him more time for artistic work outside in the wilderness. In 1946, Adams received money from a Guggenheim

a number from 0 to 10 according to its brightness: light zones get high numbers and dark zones get low numbers. The photographer chooses the key element in the zone and assigns it a zone number, and then all the other light levels of the picture fall into place.

By adjusting the exposure of the camera (and sometimes using other lighting techniques, depending on the scene) a photographer can change the brightness of that key element in the photograph and make it pop or fade accordingly in the final image.

When developing such a picture from film, the photographer can use even more techniques to achieve the different brightness zones that were originally visualized. Adams was a perfectionist when it came to developing his own photographs, and always used the Zone System to bring out all the light and dark pieces of a picture. Ideally, he tried to get the full range of brightness zones in each image.

In Adams's book *Examples: The Making of 40 Photographs*, published in 1983, he explains his use of the Zone System and how to apply it. The system is still widely used today in both film and digital photography.

Fellowship that allowed him to take a small break from his commercial work. The Guggenheim Fellowships are grants designed for mid-career artists. They have been awarded every year since 1925. Adams welcomed the relief. Funded by the fellowship, he traveled the country photographing the national parks. The fellowship was renewed in 1948 and again in 1958.

In addition to commercial photography, Adams began teaching his skill to help make ends meet. In 1941, along with fellow teacher Fred Archer, he developed the Zone System of Photography, a technique to determine the best exposure times for a photograph. It was his first major instructive writing on photography, and more would follow. In 1945, he helped set up the photography department at the California School of Fine Arts and taught there for some time. He quickly discovered that the only thing he could teach was his technique; he could not teach his artistic vision.

Soon Adams gave up teaching at the school because he found it very time consuming. He taught on and off for the rest of his life and continued to write instruction-oriented books. Adams's successful photography textbooks include *The Camera and the Lens* and *The Negative* in 1948; *Natural Light Photography* in 1952; and *Artificial Light Photography* in 1956.

In 1955, Adams began teaching photography workshops at Yosemite—a setting and schedule that he greatly preferred. That same year, a new photography exhibit at Yosemite directly linked his art and conservation work for the first time.

THE EXHIBIT AT YOSEMITE

In 1955, a photographic exhibit of 32 photographers (including Adams) opened at Yosemite. The exhibit, called *This is the American Earth,* marked the first time Adams's artistic work had been clearly exhibited to raise awareness of conservation issues. A 1955 flyer advertising the exhibit explained it this way:

> The purpose of this exhibit *This is the American Earth* is not only to present the natural scene in terms of National Parks and

wilderness areas, but also to give perspective to the whole vast pattern of conservation. We hope this will aid in a more specific appreciation of parks and wilderness and encourage constructive action on their behalf. The exhibit suggests the enormous inspirational potential of the natural scene, and pleads for wise forest protection and use, for the cautious building of dams, for understanding of management of the soil, and for the protection of wildlife. It strives for continuation of the wilderness mood, the spiritual experience of young and old in the presence of nature.

After its run at Yosemite, the Smithsonian Institution sent *This is the American Earth* on a tour of museums in the United States. By all accounts, the exhibit was a success.

Adams and a close friend, Nancy Newhall, put together the exhibit. Newhall was a photography critic, avid writer, and long-time friend of Adams. To create the exhibit, Adams collected the photographs, Newhall wrote the text, and the Sierra Club provided its LeConte Lodge at Yosemite to house the exhibition. Yet it was the accompanying book—published four years later by the Sierra Club—that became the real conservation tool.

THE EXHIBIT BECOMES A BOOK

In 1960, David Brower and the Sierra Club transformed the *This is the American Earth* photography exhibit into a popular coffee table book. The pictures, combined with Newhall's poetic, conservation-minded text, made for a widely read and well-regarded conservation tool.

The book gained fame at about the same time as the publication of Rachel Carson's famous book *Silent Spring,* which discussed the effects of chemicals and pesticides on the environment. Though *Silent Spring* is often cited as the book that helped launch the modern environmental movement, many experts credit the book *This is the American Earth* as another powerful motivator of the time.

According to many sources, William O. Douglas, a justice on the Supreme Court from 1939 to 1975, called *This is the American Earth*

Adams, shown beside his camera in March 1961, encouraged people to appreciate the land through his photo exhibitions and books, at the same time as conservationist Rachel Carson.

"one of the great statements in the history of conservation." In 1992, the Sierra Club reissued the book and recreated the exhibit at the Ansel Adams Center in San Francisco as part of its hundredth anniversary celebration. The exhibit traveled to the American Museum of Natural History in New York City and throughout Japan in 1993.

Adams and Newhall published seven books together; *This is the American Earth* was by far the most popular, and arguably the most influential. By the time he was 60, Adams's work as a photographer and as a conservationist was well respected nationwide. He finally began to enjoy some recognition for his work.

Presidents and Prizes

In 1963, the M.H. de Young Museum in San Francisco hosted an exhibition of Ansel Adams's lifetime of photographs called *The Eloquent Light*. That same year, Nancy Newhall put together a book about Adams by the same name. *The Eloquent Light* marked the beginning of the end of Adams's photographic career. Arguably, as his photographic creativity slowed, his power to raise awareness on conservation issues only got stronger. High-level lawmakers and presidents listened to him.

Adams was not an expert on the environment in any technical way. He was not a biologist. He was not a geologist. He was not a scientist at all. Yet during the last two decades of his life, he met with four presidents by invitation—Lyndon B. Johnson, Gerald Ford, Jimmy Carter, and Ronald Reagan—specifically to talk about conserving the nation's wild places.

Adams's ability to influence political thinking with his words and photographs was powerful. The recognition of this power became clear in the last decades of his life when a series of awards came rolling in.

Adams, shown in 1965 looking to set up a photo in Yosemite National Park, was considered an influential artist by politicians who had similar goals of saving the environment.

MEETING PRESIDENT LYNDON B. JOHNSON

In 1965, President Lyndon B. Johnson asked Adams and Nancy Newhall to put together a book to reflect his own interest in the environment. Johnson, it seems, knew how influential Adams's photographs could be in bringing attention to conservation causes.

Lyndon B. Johnson had been the vice president under President John F. Kennedy. When President Kennedy was assassinated in 1963, Johnson became president. He was then elected as president in 1964, and served until January 1969. During his presidency, he

NANCY NEWHALL (1908–1974)

Nancy Newhall was a photographer, critic, writer, and conservationist who helped make photography a legitimate form of art. She was decades ahead of her time in her prolific writings about visual literacy and television, but she is best known for writing the pro-conservation text to accompany Ansel Adams's images in the Sierra Club's *This is the American Earth* in 1960.

Newhall's husband, Beaumont Newhall, was the first photography curator at the Museum of Modern Art in New York City. When he was on active duty in the Air Force during World War II, Newhall substituted for him as photography curator from 1942 to 1945. Through this and her own work, she became a well-known name in the field.

Together, the Newhalls were close confidants and critics of Adams. He often wrote them letters seeking opinions of his work, sharing his thoughts on photography, and seeking direction when he was stressed or stuck on something. For example, Adams confides to Nancy in this letter from 1951, as printed in *Letters and Images:*

designed a set of domestic legislation known as the Great Society, which supported new programs for education, medical care, transportation, and civil rights. At the same time, he increased U.S. involvement in the unpopular Vietnam War, and was not a presidential candidate in the 1968 election.

Adams met with President Johnson twice at the White House and the two talked about their shared interest in conservation. Adams found President Johnson impressive and intelligent. The resulting book, called *A More Beautiful America,* included Adams's photographs printed opposite excerpts from President Johnson's

Dear Nancy,

The spirit is willing but the so-and-so is feeble! I am pooped, peaked and pallid—batty, busted and brown—foolish, flatulent, and fatigued! What I need right now is a good long session with you. A breakdown of all the swell letters and ideas; a plan for the future . . . I never felt more disorganized in my life! . . . Wish I could sit down in the new house with you and B [Beaumont] and just relax!

Love, Ansel

This letter is just one of many Adams wrote to Nancy over the years. Still, Nancy did have a career of her own to manage.

In 2009, the Museum of Photographic Arts in San Diego put together an exhibition entitled "Nancy Newhall: A Literacy of Images" to celebrate the hundredth anniversary of her birth. The exhibit contained more than 120 photographs from Newhall and others, samples of her writings, and examples of her role legitimizing photography as a fine art. An abbreviated online version of the exhibit can be found through the Traditional Fine Arts Organization at www.tfaoi.com/aa/8aa/8aa214.htm.

President Lyndon B. Johnson and his wife Lady Bird, along with their dog Yuki, enjoy the great outdoors on their Texas Ranch in 1967. Johnson was among many presidents who respected Adams's work.

many speeches on the environment. The following is one excerpt that appears in the book, taken from a speech President Johnson gave to Congress in February 1965, urging members to protect wild lands in the United States:

> It is not the classic conservation of protection and development, but creative conservation of restoration and innovation. Its concern is not with nature alone, but with the total relation between man and the world around him. Its object is not just man's welfare but the dignity of his spirit. Above all, we must maintain the chance for contact with beauty. When that chance dies, a light dies in all of us. It is our children who will bear the burden of

our neglect. We owe it to them to keep that from happening. For once the battle is lost, once our natural splendor is destroyed, it can never be recaptured. And once man can no longer walk with beauty or wonder at nature, his spirit will wither and his sustenance be wasted.

A More Beautiful America is no longer in print. Copies are considered collector's items and are sold for nearly $3,000.

THE CONSERVATION SERVICE AWARD

In 1968, under the direction of President Johnson, Adams received the Conservation Service Award from the Department of the Interior, the agency ultimately in charge of the country's national parks. According to the Sierra Club Web page on the life of Ansel Adams, the award was given to him "in recognition of [his] many years of distinguished work as a photographer, artist, interpreter, and conservationist, a role in which [his] efforts have been of profound importance in the conservation of our great natural resources."

RESIGNATION FROM THE SIERRA CLUB

In 1971, Adams quietly resigned from his position on the Sierra Club's board of directors. Adams knew that the club was growing nationwide, and that his contribution to conservation was different from that of the other members of the board. In a letter dated September 13, 1971, to Sierra Club President Ray Sherwin, Adams wrote:

> With deep regret, but with firm conviction that my action is correct and for the general good of the Sierra Club, I herewith present my resignation as a member of the Board of Directors (a position I have been honored to hold since 1934). My resignation should take effect immediately . . . .
>
> The Sierra Club has developed into a large and potent national organization. It is imperative that the governing body—the

directors—be composed of experts in the important fields of law, politics, science, and finance. I do not fit in any of these categories; my contributions have been (and will continue) in the fields of creative photography and the interpretation of aesthetic appreciation of the natural scene.

I am confident that I can accomplish as much, or more, off the board—as a regular member of the club.

As promised, Adams remained a member of the Sierra Club. He knew his contribution to conservation was not typical, and he continued his conservation efforts in his own ways.

MEETING PRESIDENT GERALD FORD

Gerald Ford was the vice president under President Richard Nixon. When President Nixon resigned in 1974, Ford became president and served until January 1977. President Ford was in office when the Vietnam War ended, and presided over the worst economy since the Great Depression. He was defeated for re-election in 1976 by Democrat Jimmy Carter.

In 1975, Adams visited President Gerald Ford in the White House to give him a copy of his photograph *Clearing Winter Storm*. The Fords had received a copy of Adams's most recent book, *Images 1923–1974*, from an art dealer and had requested a copy of their favorite Adams image to hang in the White House. Adams seized the opportunity to express his concern to the president over the deterioration of the country's national parks.

Adams presented President Ford with a document titled *New Initiatives for the National Parks*. The memo, authored by Adams and reprinted in his 1985 autobiography, was a numbered to-do list for the president that was designed to soften the human impact on the wild places of the United States.

Though Adams found President Ford to be cordial, attentive, and genuine, only minor steps followed his memo. Adams visited

President Gerald Ford's daughter, Susan, learns about photography from Adams at his gallery near Yosemite National Park in June 1975.

KEY POINTS OF ADAMS'S MEMO TO FORD	
New Initiatives for the National Parks By Ansel Adams, 1975	Background
1. Redefinition of the meaning of parks, and the basic purposes of the system.	Adams was deeply concerned about the deterioration of the national parks.
2. A Presidential Commission to thoroughly study and modernize the organization, personnel, and attitudes of the National Park System.	
3. A major review of concessions policy and management, developing non-profit, public trustee foundations as the optimum approach to best serving the public and the parks.	Adams greatly disliked the food stands and gift stores found in or near the visitor centers of the parks.
4. Reduction of man's physical impact on prime areas such as Yosemite Valley and replacement of automobiles by alternative transportation systems in most parks and monuments.	Adams felt the Tioga Pass modernization had forever destroyed a piece of Yosemite and strongly opposed too many roads and cars in the parks.

President Ford in the White House several times after this first meeting, and the Fords visited the Adams house for lunch after his presidency ended.

MEETING PRESIDENT JIMMY CARTER

Jimmy Carter served as president from 1977 to 1981. He is a strong advocate for human rights and established a new national energy policy during his presidency that stressed energy conservation.

New Initiatives for the National Parks By Ansel Adams, 1975	Background
5. New emphasis on preservation and environmental responsibilities. Improved park interpretation, stressing natural values and contemporary awareness.	"Environmentalism" was still a new idea in 1975. Adams wanted to bring it to the National Park Service.
6. Improved National Park Service performance in realizing and expanding compliance with the Wilderness Act.	The Wilderness Act defined wilderness in the United States. When signed by President Johnson in 1964, about 9 million acres (3.6 million ha) were protected.
7. Urgent Presidential intervention to prevent any Office of Management and Budget reductions in proposed Park Service Budget and staffing levels.	The National Park Service budget had been reduced during the Nixon Administration (1969 to 1974).
8. Presidential level review of all areas of future park or reserve potential. This generation may have the last chance to save essential lands for future generations.	Typical of Adams's passion, this last point includes a plea to save the wild lands he so loved.

President Carter won the Nobel Peace Prize in 2002, the only president to receive the prize after leaving office.

In 1979, Carter invited Adams to make official portraits of himself and Vice President Walter Mondale for the National Portrait Gallery at the Smithsonian. Then in 1980, President Carter awarded Adams with the Presidential Medal of Freedom.

The Presidential Medal of Freedom is the highest award that a civilian can receive, and is given only by the president to one or more individuals each year. According to the White House Web site, the

LATE LIFE EXHIBITIONS

During the last two decades of Adams's life, exhibitions commemorating his photographic work became popular around the world. Adams often had nothing to do with the development of these exhibitions, but by now it was clear that he would be remembered as the country's great photographer, and a huge advocate for its national parks.

A SELECTION OF ADAMS'S RETROSPECTIVE EXHIBITS	
Year	Exhibit
1963	"An Eloquent Light" M.H. de Young Museum, San Francisco
1972	"Ansel Adams: Recollected Moments" San Francisco Museum of Modern Art
1974	Ansel Adams work The Victoria and Albert Museum, London
1974	"Singular Images" San Francisco Museum of Modern Art
1977	"Ansel Adams and the West" Museum of Modern Art, New York
1978	"Ansel Adams: 50 Years of Portraits" Friends of Photography, Carmel, California
1982	"The Unknown Ansel Adams" Friends of Photography, Carmel, California
1983	Ansel Adams work National Museum of Beijing

Adams sets up his camera on a bluff overlooking the Pacific Ocean in this May 1981 image.

Medal of Freedom "is awarded to individuals who make an especially meritorious contribution to the security or national interests of the United States, world peace, cultural or other significant public or private endeavors."

When President Carter gave the Medal of Freedom to Adams, the accompanying citation recognized Adams's contribution to conservation of the nation's wild lands. It read:

> At one with the power of the American landscape, and renowned for the patient skill and timeless beauty of his work, photographer Ansel Adams has been a visionary in his efforts to preserve this country's wild and scenic areas, both on film and on Earth. Drawn to the beauty of nature's monuments, he is regarded by environmentalists as a monument himself, and by photographers as a

national institution. It is through his foresight and fortitude that so much of America has been saved for future Americans.

MEETING PRESIDENT RONALD REAGAN

Ronald Reagan was the Republican president from 1981 to 1989. He is remembered for "Reaganomics," a sweeping economic policy that included cutting taxes and reducing government spending and regulation. He is also remembered for his strong anti-communist, pro-military views.

In 1983, President Reagan invited Adams to talk about why Adams hated him so much. Adams was very outspoken in his

Adams poses with his viewfinder camera at a party celebrating the fortieth anniversary of his famous photograph *Moonrise Over Hernandez, N.M.* in October 1981.

dislike of Reagan, and had said so in many interviews and magazine articles. Adams agreed to meet with President Reagan in the hopes that the president would listen to his conservation concerns.

Adams and President Reagan talked about conservation for almost an hour (Adams had been told to expect only 15 minutes). According to Adams's autobiography, they agreed on only one point: the value of nuclear energy for the future. Adams felt the meeting was tense, and that President Reagan failed to discuss or challenge his opinions on environmental issues. The two did not meet again.

A PEACEFUL DEATH

On April 22, 1984—Earth Day—Adams died of heart failure at a hospital near his home in Carmel, California, at the age of 82. His death made the national news on television and in newspapers. His 50-year career resulted in more than 35 books and portfolios, hundreds of photography exhibitions, and immeasurable public appreciation of the beauty of the country's wild lands.

Six months after his death, Congress named some of Adams's favorite wilderness areas after him. Six months after that, they named one of his favorite mountains after him.

The Accidental
Conservationist

Arguably, the popularity of Ansel Adams the photographer has only grown since his death in 1984. Fewer than 10 years after his death, according to *Ansel Adams: A Biography* (1996), Adams's calendars alone had sold more than 3.4 million copies. An original Adams photograph could easily cost more than $50,000—if you can find one for sale.

As Adams's friend and biographer Mary Street Alinder wrote in her 1996 biography of him, "Ansel Adams did not truly die on April 22, 1984. With great artists, the art lives on. Ansel's photographs have proliferated, perhaps even saturated the world, since his death." In fact, it's hard to go into a shopping mall or a card store in the United States without seeing at least one of Adams's now-famous black and white images.

What's harder to argue is the popularity of Ansel Adams the conservationist, whose legacy is not always so obvious. He had set out to be an artist and help validate and establish photography as an art form. Without meaning to, he became something of an accidental conservationist to those familiar with his non-photography work. He didn't set out to preserve the nation's natural beauty, but by preserving that beauty in his photographs, Adams did exactly that.

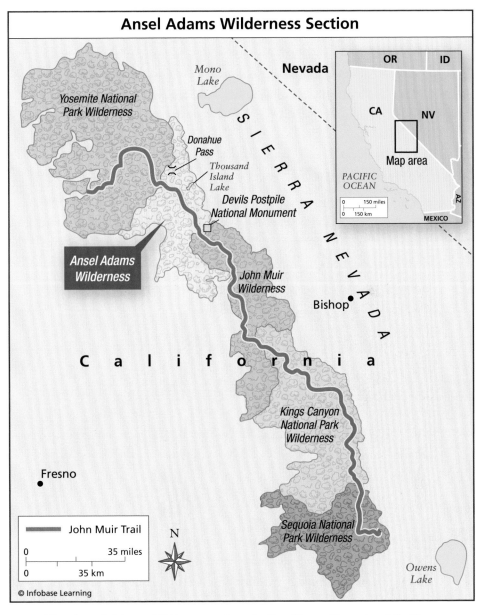

Ansel Adams Wilderness Section

The Ansel Adams Wilderness Area in the Sierra Nevada of California spans 231,533 acres (93,698 hectares).

ARTISTIC LEGACY

Today, Adams's artistic legacy is preserved in more than one place. His images and books are reprinted and sold in stores throughout the world. Many of his original photographs—the photographic prints that he made himself—hang in the White House and in galleries, museums, and private homes around the world. Two main libraries now hold much of his original work. The photography workshops that Adams taught during his summers at Yosemite continue today as well.

The Center for Creative Photography at the University of Arizona

The Center for Creative Photography (CCP)—a special section of the library at the University of Arizona in Tucson—holds a large portion of Adams's artistic archive. According to its Web site, the CCP "actively collects, preserves, interprets, manages, and makes available materials that are essential to understanding photography and its history." Here, the work of Adams and more than 2,000 other photographers is stored and cared for.

In 1975, Adams co-founded the CCP with $75,000 and the archives of four fellow photographers: Wynn Bullock, Harry Callahan, Aaron Siskind, and Frederick Sommer. Every year since then, the CCP has added one to three new photography archives, making it the largest archive for twentieth-century North American photographers in the nation.

The archives include photographs, negatives, albums, work prints, manuscripts, audio-visual materials, contact sheets, correspondence, and memorabilia, totaling about 3.8 million items. Most of these items can be viewed in the CCP gallery, in specified research rooms, or online. The CCP is open to the public and features a changing exhibit. The entire CCP Ansel Adams archive—containing 2,664 photographs—can be viewed online at http://ccp.uair.arizona.edu/item/4538.

Virginia Adams stands in front of her husband's photograph *Monolith, The Face of Half Dome* in 1985. She is holding his post-humous autobiography, which contains images that had not been published before his death.

The National Archives Still Picture Branch

The National Archives Still Picture Branch in College Park, Maryland, holds 226 photographs of national parks taken, signed, and captioned by Adams himself. Most of these photographs were part of a project that started in 1941, when the National Park Service hired Adams to take pictures of the parks for display in the Department of the Interior building in Washington, D.C.

The project was stopped during World War II and never officially completed. The National Park Service still owns Adams's photographs for the project, including images from the Grand Canyon, Grand Teton, Kings Canyon, Mesa Verde, Rocky Mountain,

Adams took this dramatic image of Canyon de Chelly in Arizona from a mountaintop for the National Park Service.

Yellowstone, Yosemite, Carlsbad Caverns, Glacier, and Zion national parks; Death Valley, Saguaro, and Canyon de Chelly national monuments, plus others.

Adams's popular image of Old Faithful, a geyser in Yellowstone National Park, erupting against a dark sky was also created for the National Park Service's project.

On March 10, 2010, Secretary of the Interior Ken Salazar completed the project that had begun more than 70 years before. On that day, Salazar revealed some of Adams's national parks photographs, which are now hanging as a mural display in the Department of the Interior's office building in Washington, D.C. The murals are intended to honor both Adams's and Ickes's work, according to the department's Web site. Adams's national parks photographs can be viewed and ordered online through the National Archives at www.archives.gov/research/ansel-adams.

Photography Workshops in Yosemite

For more than 25 years, Adams taught photography workshops in Yosemite each summer. Over his lifetime he taught thousands of students. Although Adams knew he could not teach his artistic vision, he could teach his technique, including his use of visualization and the Zone System. And he taught it often.

Today, the Ansel Adams Gallery in Yosemite teaches about a dozen different photography workshops during the summer for all levels and types of photography, just as Adams did. You can learn more about the classes offered at the Ansel Adams Gallery through its Web site at www.anseladams.com.

CONSERVATION LEGACY

Adams's conservation legacy is difficult to measure, but his influence on conservation in the United States certainly lives on in his photographs. Adams's photographs of the nation's wild places showed people and politicians places they had never seen before—places they might never see for themselves. Because of Adams's unique artistic and technical skill, those photographs were almost as beautiful as the wild lands themselves.

In the year following his death, Congress took immediate action to rename two wild places near Yosemite in his honor. Two major conservation awards from the organizations he worked most closely with—the Sierra Club and the Wilderness Society—now bear his

MATTHEW ADAMS (1967–)

Matthew Adams is the grandson of Ansel Adams, and the current president of the Ansel Adams Gallery, a shop located in Yosemite that sells authorized reproductions of Adams's work. The Ansel Adams Gallery was originally Best's Studio, the small art shop and studio first owned by Ansel Adams's father-in-law, Harry Best. That makes Matthew Adams the fourth generation in his family to operate the shop.

Yet the shop has a problem. Original photographs by Ansel Adams are still very much in demand, according to the gallery. Because Adams has been dead for several decades, there are a limited number of originals to be sold, and they can cost tens of thousands of dollars each. The shop has trouble keeping up with customer demand.

As a result, Matthew Adams is leading an effort to make digital copies of Ansel Adams's original photographs and sell them to art collectors at more affordable prices. But these aren't just any old digital copies. The goal is to create digital copies that are just as good—even to collectors—as the original Adams images. Matthew Adams, who is an expert on his grandfather's work, says it's difficult even for him to tell the difference between the digital copies and the originals.

Although Ansel Adams lived and worked largely before the age of digital photography, he admitted late in life that if he had been a young artist when computers first enabled photographers to manipulate digital photographs fairly easily, he would certainly have explored digital photography more. In a way, Matthew Adams is exploring that possibility for him.

Matthew Adams explains the digital process he uses and shows some copies of his digital work in a video on the Adams gallery blog. For more information, visit http://theanseladamsgallery.blogspot.com/2009/03/matthew-adams-on-ansel-adams-gallery.html.

It is at this point that the John Muir Trail crosses a stream in the Ansel Adams Wilderness. Mount Ritter and Banner Peak are in the distance.

name as well. Each namesake is a small reminder of Adams's conservation legacy.

The Ansel Adams Wilderness Area

The Ansel Adams Wilderness Area is a 231,533-acre (93,698-ha) piece of land nestled between Yosemite National Park and the John Muir Wilderness Area in California. It is an area about the size of Cape Cod, Massachusetts. Part of the area was originally preserved in 1964 as the Minaret Wilderness. The Minarets are a series of jagged mountain peaks south of the High Sierra.

When Adams died in 1984, California senators Alan Cranston and Pete Wilson persuaded Congress to pass the California Wilderness

Act that year, nearly doubling the protected land and renaming it the Ansel Adams Wilderness Area. "Wilderness" land is officially part of the National Wilderness Preservation System, which means that these places are doubly protected. They must remain undeveloped, with no big roads or human habitation of any kind. In addition, wilderness areas are managed in a way that preserves their natural conditions as best as possible—just as Adams had always fought for.

Today, the Sierra Club leads many different summer Outings to the Ansel Adams Wilderness Area each year.

Mount Ansel Adams

On April 23, 1985—one year and one day after the death of Ansel Adams—the United States Geological Survey officially named a jagged mountain peak in Yosemite "Mount Ansel Adams." The peak, at 11,760 feet (3,584 meters), lies on the southern border of the park alongside the Ansel Adams Wilderness, and is at the head of the Lyell Fork of the Merced River.

According to the Ansel Adams Gallery online, the peak was in one of Adams's favorite areas in Yosemite, and he affectionately called the unnamed mountain "the tower" on the many occasions that he visited the area himself. Adams took many photographs of that mountain.

In 1934, while leading a Sierra Club Outing to Lyell Fork, Adams and his group climbed the peak. Over the evening campfire, according to the gallery, the group decided that the peak should be named after their leader. But because mountains could not be named after living people, they had to wait until Adams's death to get their wish.

The Ansel Adams Award

According to the Sierra Club Web site on club awards, the Ansel Adams Award officially "honors an individual who has made superlative use of still photography to further a conservation cause." The award was established in 1971. The Sierra Club was arguably the first organization to understand the conservation power of Adams's work. This award encourages more conservation through photography.

ANSEL ADAMS IN BRIEF

Ansel Adams's lifetime of work—both as a photographer and as a conservationist—is difficult to quantify. No one can really count the number of people who saw an Adams photograph and were moved to visit, conserve, respect, or learn more about the country's wild places.

He didn't discover anything new. He didn't explain anything scientific. Nor did he save any particular piece of land all by himself. Yet Adams got people's attention. People looked at his photographs and wanted to learn more about the places they saw. He had a powerful voice in the last decades of his life. But Adams never tried to tell people what to think about his photographs. He just made beautiful photographs of wild places, explained what was in them, and let others decide for themselves.

His influence on the country's attitude towards conservation—through his photographs and writings—is undeniable. Looking at the sheer popularity of his work and the number of things he accomplished makes it clear that he was an influential conservationist.

Joshua Wolfe, for example, was the 2009 winner of the Ansel Adams Award, and is using photography to show how climate change is affecting people and the planet. His photographs documenting climate change can be viewed on his Web site at www.joshuawolfe.com.

The Ansel Adams Award for Conservation

According to the Wilderness Society Web site on Historical Heroes, the Ansel Adams Award for Conservation goes to "a current or former federal official who has been a fervent advocate of conservation." The award was first given in 1980; past recipients include

ANSEL ADAMS'S ACCOMPLISHMENTS IN NUMBERS

Number of photographs taken and sold	millions
Number of letters written for conservation	thousands
Number of photography students taught	thousands
Number of national park photographs	300 or more
Number of years on the Sierra Club board	37
Number of books and portfolios published	35 or more
Number of U.S. presidents who met with Adams	4
Number of Guggenheim Fellowships received	3
Number of awards received from U.S. presidents	2
Number of wild places bearing his name	2

former secretary of the interior Stewart Udall and former president Jimmy Carter.

Although Adams was most involved with the Sierra Club in his conservation work, he wrote often for the Wilderness Society's member magazine *Living Wilderness*. In 1984, Adams gave the society 75 of his original prints for display in the group's Washington, D.C., offices. The prints are still there today.

In 2009, Democrat Senator Jeff Bingaman of New Mexico received the Ansel Adams Award for Conservation for his environmental leadership, particularly in passing a bill in March 2009 that protected 2 million acres (0.9 ha) of wilderness in nine different

Michael Adams admires his father's work on exhibit at St. Louis's Mildred Lane Kemper Art Museum at Washington University in May 2007. He fondly remembers being as young as 8 years old when he would hike with his father and carry his gear as the photographer took some of his most famous photos.

states. It was the biggest public land protection bill in a generation, according to the Wilderness Society.

THE ACCIDENTAL CONSERVATIONIST

Carl Pope was the executive director of the Sierra Club until 2010, spending almost two decades in that position. Pope believed that Ansel Adams lived during an important time for conservation in U.S. history, a time when the country had to decide whether or not wild places should be valued and preserved.

In the decade before Adams was born, the U.S. frontier unofficially closed. The "frontier" was any land unsettled by non-Native Americans, generally located in the West, that the U.S. government made available for development and homesteading. By the time Ansel Adams was born in 1902, Americans had settled throughout the entire nation, and there was no land farther West that could be dubbed an unsettled frontier. The frontier was closed.

During this time, as Pope told documentary filmmaker Ric Burns in *Ansel Adams: A Documentary Film* (2002), Americans had big decisions to make about what they wanted the country to be like. "Who were we going to be, now that we didn't have a frontier anymore?" Pope asks.

Pope argues that Adams's photographs provided one answer: that wildness did not end with the frontier. There were still wild places in the United States worth seeing and protecting. As Pope says, "We wanted a place that was still wild." Adams's photographs showed people that those places were still out there.

Ansel Adams never set out to become a conservationist. He just loved the land. Nor did he set out to take photographs for conservation purposes. He only took photographs for the sake of the art. But when his two passions accidentally converged to help the environment, he said that this made him very happy. "I never went out and made an important photograph for conservation purposes," Adams explained late in his life in a video presented in *Ansel Adams at 100,* an exhibit put together by the San Francisco Museum of Modern Art. "I made the photograph as a photograph—personal expression. Then I find, if it's used for the cause, why, I'm very happy."

How to Get Involved

These organizations provide resources to gain information and get involved in conservation issues.

The Blue Earth Alliance

www.blueearth.org

The Blue Earth Alliance supports using documentary photographs for social change. The organization partnered with the Ansel Adams Gallery in 2009 to launch a new exhibit called "Changing Earth: Photographer's Call to Action" at the Mumm Napa Fine Photography Gallery in Rutherford, California.

International Conservation Photography Awards

www.icpawards.com

This conservation-themed photography contest for amateurs and professionals works towards the "advancement of photography as a unique medium capable of bringing awareness and preservation to our environment through art." The contest is open to any photographer anywhere in the world, and there is a special student category for photographers under age 18.

The Sierra Club

www.sierraclub.org

There are multiple ways to get involved with the Sierra Club and help support the ongoing causes that Ansel Adams worked for in his lifetime. Some possible actions include signing up for the email newsletter, going on a Sierra Club Outing, and becoming a member.

The Wilderness Society

http://wilderness.org

The Wilderness Society is active in the southwestern United States and at the national level. It works on many of Adams's priority conservation issues, including wilderness areas, roadless forests, and more.

Yosemite Youth Conservation Corps

http://www.nps.gov/yose/parkmgmt/ycc.htm

Through the Yosemite Youth Conservation Corps, young people ages 15 to 18 can live and work at Yosemite National Park during the summer. Most work takes place outside and is physically demanding. Projects may include trail and campground maintenance and building fences.

Chronology

1902	Ansel Adams is born February 20 in San Francisco, California.
1906	The San Francisco Earthquake occurs; followed by three days of fire.
1907	The Adams family loses much of its family fortune in the post-quake financial panic.
1908	Mary Bray (Aunt Mary) comes to live with the Adams family.
1914	Ansel Adams stops going to school; he begins learning to play the piano and practicing for his intended career as a concert pianist.
1915	The Panama-Pacific Exposition comes to San Francisco; Adams gets a yearlong pass to the exposition from his father.
1916	Adams visits Yosemite National Park for the first time and takes his first photos.
1917	He begins work developing film and making prints for a neighbor's business.
1920	Adams spends the first of four summers working as the custodian at the LeConte Memorial Lodge in Yosemite.
1921	He meets Virginia Best in Yosemite and starts practicing on her father's piano during the summers.
1922	His first photographs and article on the Lyell Fork of the Merced River published in the Sierra Club *Bulletin*.
1925	Adams decides to become a concert pianist and purchases a Mason and Hamlin grand piano.

1927	Adams publishes first portfolio, *Parmelian Prints of the High Sierras;* he takes the photograph *Monolith, the Face of Half Dome,* which he considered his first fully visualized image.
1928	Adams marries Virginia Best in Yosemite; he has his first one-man exhibit held at the Sierra Club in San Francisco.
1930	Adams becomes completely dedicated to photography after meeting photographer Paul Strand; publishes *Taos Pueblo.*
1931	Adams has an exhibition of 60 prints at the Smithsonian Institution.
1932	He co-founds the straight photography group f/64.
1933	Adams opens his own gallery in San Francisco; his son, Michael, is born.
1934	He is elected to the board of directors of the Sierra Club.
1935	His daughter, Anne, is born.
1936	Adams opens a one-man exhibition in New York City; he starts lobbying Congress on behalf of the Sierra Club for the creation of Kings Canyon National Park.
1937	His darkroom in Yosemite burns and destroys 20 percent of his negatives; the family moves to Yosemite and takes over Best's Studio.
1938	*Sierra Nevada: The John Muir Trail* is published.
1939	Adams has a major exhibition at the San Francisco Museum of Modern Art.
1940	Adams helps found Department of Photography at New York's Museum of Modern Art; Kings Canyon National Park is established with help from Adams and the Sierra Club; Adams publishes the *Illustrated*

Guide to Yosemite with Virginia Adams as co-author; he teaches his first photography workshop in Yosemite.

1941 Adams develops Zone System of photography, a technique of exposure and development control.

1946 He receives a Guggenheim Fellowship to photograph national parks; he publishes *Illustrated Guide to Yosemite Valley* with Virginia Adams.

1948 The Guggenheim Fellowship renewed.

1949 Adams becomes consultant for Polaroid Corporation.

1951 Charles Adams dies.

1953 Adams creates a *Life* magazine photo essay on the Mormons in Utah.

1955 The Ansel Adams Yosemite Workshop begins as an annual event.

1958 Adams receives third Guggenheim Fellowship.

1960 Adams publishes *This is the American Earth.*

1962 Adams builds a home and studio overlooking the Pacific Ocean in Carmel, California; he produces most of the fine prints of his career in this place over the next two decades.

1963 *The Eloquent Light* exhibit runs at the de Young Museum in San Francisco; *The Eloquent Light,* the book, is published.

1965 Adams is named to President Johnson's environmental task force; he meets with the president to talk about conservation.

1968 He receives the Conservation Service Award from the Department of the Interior.

1971 Adams resigns from the Sierra Club board of directors after 37 years of service.

1975	Adams helps found Center for Creative Photography at University of Arizona; his archives are established there.
1980	Adams is awarded Presidential Medal of Freedom by President Jimmy Carter.
1984	Adams dies on April 22, Earth Day.
1984	Congress establishes the Ansel Adams Wilderness Area south of Yosemite.
1985	Mount Ansel Adams is named in his honor.

Glossary

abstract photography   Using forms, colors, and lines to create a photographic image

composition   The placement of visual elements in a work of art

contrast   The difference between the light and dark pieces of a photograph

darkroom   A room that can be made completely dark for the processing of light-sensitive, photographic materials

Department of the Interior   Part of the federal government responsible for the management and conservation of federal lands

digital photography   Uses digital technology to create photographic images

Earth Day   A holiday to inspire awareness and appreciation for the Earth's environment; it began in 1970.

exposure   The total amount of light allowed to enter the lens when taking a photograph

film photography   Film is a sheet of light-sensitive plastic that, when exposed to light, captures a photographic image; the image is then transferred to paper or other surfaces using a chemical process in the darkroom.

frontier   Any land in the United States unsettled by non-Native Americans prior to about 1900; generally located toward the West, it was made available by the U.S. government for development and homesteading.

granite   A type of rock common in Yosemite; it forms when lava erupts from a volcano and cools.

Group f/64   An organization founded in 1932 to advocate for straight photography

High Sierra   The California mountain ridges found roughly between 8,000 to 14,000 feet (2,438 to 4,267 m) of elevation

Kodak Box Brownie   Introduced in 1900, it was the first inexpensive, portable camera.

National Park Service The federal agency that manages all national parks, many national monuments, and other conservation and historical properties

negative An image with inverted light used to make a photographic print

Panama-Pacific International Exposition The 1915 World's Fair held in San Francisco

photodiary The name Adams gave books he made as a child composed of his early photographs mounted on paper

pictorial photography An early style of photography that sought to make photographs that looked like paintings or drawings

shutter The device on a camera that allows light to pass through the lens for a certain period of time

single-lens reflex camera A type of camera that allows a photographer to look directly through the lens when taking a picture

straight photography A style of photography that attempts to depict a scene realistically and objectively

visualization (or pre-visualization) A technique to picture the final print of a photograph—with composition and contrast—in one's head before snapping the shutter on the camera

wilderness Land that has not been altered significantly by human contact

Zone System A technique to determine the best exposure times for a photograph

Bibliography

Adams, Ansel and Mary Street Alinder. *An Autobiography*. Boston: Little, Brown and Company, 1985.

Adams, Ansel. *Examples: The Making of 40 Photographs*. Boston: Little, Brown and Company, 1989.

Alinder, Mary Street. *Ansel Adams: A Biography*. New York: Henry Holt and Company, 1996.

Alinder, Mary Street and Andrea Gray Stillman. *Ansel Adams: Letters and Images 1916–1984*. Boston: Little, Brown and Company, 1988.

The Ansel Adams Gallery. Available online. URL: http://www.anseladams. com. Accessed July 8, 2010.

Burns, Ric. *Ansel Adams: A Documentary Film*. DVD. Public Broadcasting Service *American Experience,* 2002. Film information online at http:// www.pbs.org/wgbh/amex/ansel.

DOI News. "Interior Unveils New Ansel Adams Murals." Available online. URL: http://doi.gov/news/doinews/2010_03_10_news.cfm. Accessed July 8, 2010.

Flint, Wendell D. *To Find the Biggest Tree*. Three Rivers, Calif.: Sequoia Natural History Association, 2002. Available online. URL: http://www. nps.gov/seki/naturescience/bigtrees.htm. Accessed July 8, 2010.

Gherman, Beverly. *Ansel Adams: America's Photographer*. New York: Little, Brown and Company, 2002.

Johnson, Lyndon B. "Beautification Act Speech." 1965. LBJ Library and Museum: LBJ for Kids! Available online. URL: http://www.lbjlib.utexas. edu/johnson/lbjforkids/enviro_legacy.shtm. Accessed July 8, 2010.

Mission 66. "Modern Architecture in the National Parks." Available online. URL: http://www.mission66.com. Accessed July 8, 2010.

Russel, John. "Ansel Adams, Photographer, is Dead." *New York Times,* April 24, 1984. Available online. URL: http://www.nytimes.com/ learning/general/onthisday/bday/0220.html. Accessed July 8, 2010.

San Francisco Museum of Modern Art. *Ansel Adams at 100.* August 2001. Available online. URL: http://www.sfmoma.org/multimedia/videos/113. Accessed July 8, 2010.

The Sierra Club. "History: Ansel Adams." Available online. URL: http://www.sierraclub.org/history/anseladams. Accessed July 8, 2010.

The Sierra Club. "LeConte Memorial Lodge." Available online. URL: http://www.sierraclub.org/education/leconte/history/this_is_the_american_earth.asp. Accessed July 8, 2010.

Turnage, Robert. "Ansel Adams: The Role of the Artist in the Environmental Movement." The Wilderness Society, March 1980. Available online. URL: http://www.anseladams.com/Articles.asp?ID=172. Accessed July 8, 2010.

United States Geological Survey, Earthquake Hazards Program. "Historic Earthquakes." Available online. URL: http://earthquake.usgs.gov/earthquakes/states/events/1906_04_18.php. Accessed July 8, 2010.

White House Press Office. "Presidential Medal of Freedom." Available online. URL: http://www.whitehouse.gov/the_press_office/president-obama-names-medal-of-freedom-recipients. Accessed July 8, 2010.

Wood, Harold W. "The History and Meaning of LeConte Memorial Lodge." The Sierra Club, July 3, 2004. Available online. URL: http://www.sierraclub.org/education/leconte/centennial/rededication/harold_wood.asp. Accessed July 8, 2010.

Further Resources

Adams, Ansel. *Ansel Adams: An Autobiography.* New York: Little, Brown and Company, 1985, 1996.

Adams, Ansel. *Examples: The Making of 40 Photographs.* Boston: Little, Brown and Company, 1989.

Adams, Ansel, James Alinder, and John Szarkowski. *Ansel Adams: Classic Images.* New York: Little, Brown and Company, 1986.

Adams, Ansel. *Ansel Adams on his Relationship to Environmentalism.* San Francisco: San Francisco Museum of Modern Art, 2001. Available online. URL: http://www.sfmoma.org/multimedia/videos/113. Accessed July 8, 2010.

Burns, Ric. *Ansel Adams: A Documentary Film.* DVD. Public Broadcasting Service *American Experience,* 2002. Film information online at http://www.pbs.org/wgbh/amex/ansel.

Gherman, Beverly. *Ansel Adams: America's Photographer: A Biography for Young People.* New York: Little, Brown and Company, 2002.

Szarkowski, John. *Ansel Adams at 100.* New York: Little, Brown and Company, 2001.

Williams, Harold. *Ansel Adams: Photographer.* Wilmington, Mass.: Houghton Mifflin, 2005.

WEB SITES

Ansel Adams and the Sierra Club
www.sierraclub.org/history/anseladams/
Ansel Adams was a key figure in the history of the Sierra Club. Its Web site includes a description of Adams's role, influence, and legacy in the organization.

Ansel Adams Archive at the Center for Creative Photography, University of Arizona

www.creativephotography.org/education/educatorsGuides/ansel Adams

This center houses all of Ansel Adams's documents and photography equipment.

San Francisco Museum of Modern Art: Ansel Adams at 100

www.sfmoma.org/multimedia/interactive_features/22

Visit an interactive online exhibit celebrating the work and life of Ansel Adams. The site includes video clips of Ansel himself describing his photographs and conservation efforts. The online exhibit was developed along with a 2002 art exhibit on the centennial of his birth.

The Ansel Adams Gallery

www.anseladams.com

A gallery owned by the Adams family and operated out of Yosemite National Park hosts a Web site containing a full selection of Adams's work for viewing and purchase. It also features a detailed biography, anecdotes, and quotes from the man himself.

Time Magazine: Ansel Adams in Color

www.time.com/time/photogallery/0,29307,1932762,00.html

This online book of Adams's exploration of color photography includes more than a dozen color images he created.

Museum Graphics

www.anseladams.org

This online store is operated by Ansel and Virginia's daughter, Anne.

Picture Credits

Index

About the Author

KRISTA WEST has always had a soft spot for fabulous nature photography. The walls of her childhood bedroom were plastered with scenes of wild cheetahs (her favorite feline) and the nearby Cascade Mountains. But not until writing this book did she realize that those photos were more than just pretty. They had an enormous influence on her conservation-minded career and lifestyle. West holds master's degrees in journalism and earth science from Columbia University, and has written numerous nonfiction books for young adults about science and the environment.